RECORD & COMPOSE

*Creative recording with the
multitrack cassette recorder*

PETER WEST
&
DEBORAH GOLDMAN

FABER MUSIC

*in association with Faber & Faber
London and Boston*

First published in 1991 by Faber Music Ltd
in association with Faber & Faber Ltd
3 Queen Square London WC1N 3AU
Typesetting by Input Typesetting
Cover design by Studio Gerrard
Printed in England

Photographs © 1991 by Devra Applebaum.
The authors and publishers would like to thank
Holland Park School and Eltham Hill School,
whose pupils feature in the photographs.

CONTENTS

INTRODUCTION

The multitrack cassette recorder – or portastudio – is one of the most useful pieces of equipment in the classroom. It supports composing, performing and listening activities for music of any style or tradition. It can be used with any combination of electric and acoustic instruments as well as voices, and will help in work by individuals, small groups, or even whole classes.

In our experience the portastudio can actively encourage the development of pupils' compositional ideas by providing the opportunity for them to listen to, reflect on and change their work at every stage.

In this book we aim to provide a number of different starting ideas for pupils' compositions as well as some simple advice on which buttons to push! To help illustrate some of the composition projects we have included specific music examples, but we hope many pupils will wish to ignore these in favour of their own musical material.

The book falls into three parts:

Part One aims to provide a quick guided tour of the portastudio. Two short practical projects provide a gentle introduction to making the first recording while explaining what the controls are doing.

Part Two contains a collection of composition projects with ideas for follow-up work and suggestions for assessment of pupils' work.

We have also included some record-keeping sheets for pupils to fill in because we believe that regular keeping of written records throughout a composition helps pupils and teachers to keep track of the work at each stage of development, as well as providing a useful basis for evaluation and assessment.

Part Three is a reference section. The chapters on microphones and effects will help pupils and teachers get the best from any portastudio. The later chapters are aimed at teachers (and older pupils who may be considering a portastudio of their own) and offer advice on buying a portastudio, setting it up in the classroom and keeping it in good working order.

The **Glossary**, which begins the book, contains simple explanations of all those technical terms that make some manufacturers' manuals unreadable!

We hope that this book will help pupils and teachers to feel confident in using a portastudio and enable them to concentrate on the important business of making music.

Here is a list of technical terms included in this book and which you may find in your portastudio manual. For other technical terms, see Chapters 13 and 14.

Amplifier A device which increases the level (loudness) of the sound being fed in.

Analogue An electrical signal which varies continuously as the sound it is transmitting varies (in pitch, volume, etc.). Most tape recorders make analogue recordings.

Automatic Gain Control The tape recorder automatically sets the level of the recording. This is particularly *useless* for music recording as the machine will record all dynamics at the same level.

Auxiliary On a TASCAM portastudio it refers to an AUXILIARY SEND. This is a rotary dial used to send some of the sound from an input channel to an Effects Unit such as REVERB.
    On an amplifier this usually refers to an additional input for Cassette or Reel-to-Reel tape machines, CD player or TV and Video audio signal.

Bias A high frequency signal that enables magnetic recording to take place. Different types of tape need different Bias frequencies and most stereo cassette machines have settings for standard, chrome, and metal tapes. You don't have to worry about Bias on a portastudio if you use chrome tape.

Bouncing (collapsing, ping-ponging) Mixing together two or three previously recorded tracks and recording the result on to a new track. This enables the original tracks to be erased and new material recorded. Skilful bouncing can enable up to ten different layers to be recorded on to a portastudio (Chapter 11: Music from Africa).

Buss Found in a mixer, this is a signal line or route which will accept several inputs. For example, when mixing four tracks one sends them to the stereo output. The stereo output consists of two busses, the left buss and the right buss (Chapter 2).

Cannon A heavy duty plug used for microphones. The most common form has three pins although there are other varieties.

Channel An input on the mixer or portastudio.

Combo A portable amplifier and speaker within the same box. There are Guitar, Bass Guitar, and Keyboard combos available.

DBX A type of Noise Reduction to suppress the hiss present in all audio tapes.

Most portastudios use DBX type II. DBX must be by-passed on any track used to record MIDI sync but this facility is not available on all multitracks (Chapter 1).

DIN A type of plug commonly used in Europe for hi-fi equipment and now used universally for MIDI connections. Although the most common form has 5 pins they also come in 3- to 7-pin varieties.

Distortion The difference in quality between the output and input of a tape recorder, amplifier, etc. Sometimes used as an effect.

Dolby An alternative type of Noise Reduction to DBX. There are two main types of Dolby system in use, Dolby B and Dolby C, the latter being the better of the two (Chapter 1).

Echo A commonly used effect where a sound is repeated once or several times (Chapter 14).

Equalisation The means of reducing or enhancing certain frequencies or frequency bands within a sound. A simple example would be tone controls to adjust the treble and bass frequencies (Chapter 3).

Fader A slider which controls the volume of a sound.

Feedback Often unwanted, it appears as a screaming or rumbling sound and is caused by sending an output back into itself. For example, a microphone placed too near a loudspeaker will progressively re-amplify the sound causing a resonating effect to grow. To avoid microphone feedback just turn the MIC level down a little until it stops. Some forms of Feedback are useful, for example Echo and Flanging effects.

Flanging An effect often used by guitarists (Chapter 14).

Frequency A technical term for describing whether a sound is high (treble) or low (bass).

Gain *see* Trim.

Graphic Equaliser A form of equalisation where the sound range is divided into several frequency bands each with its controlling fader. Visually these faders give a graphic representation of the frequency adjustment.

Hiss Always present in analogue recording systems. Poor quality tapes will add significantly to the hiss level.

Hum Usually caused by the mains supply; consult an electrician, *don't* try to fix it yourself!

Impedance The 'amount of resistance' to a signal, measured in ohms. All porta-studios are designed to take low impedance microphones (in the 200–600 ohms range).

All audio equipment will have an ideal impedance at both input and output, and the golden rule is *never* connect a high output to a low input. This is especially important when connecting loudspeakers into a system.

Jack Plug A commonly-used plug that is available in two main sizes, and in mono and stereo versions. Most instruments use standard ¼ inch (6.25mm) mono (2 pole) jack plugs. Some of the cheaper electronic keyboards use mini (3.5mm) mono jack plugs. Stereo headphones are available with both sizes, but use stereo (3 pole) versions of the plug.

LED   Light Emitting Diode. Small green, yellow and red lights which show sound levels on tape recorders and mixers.

Line In   Sockets used to connect keyboards, synthesisers, other tape recorders, and effects units to the portastudio.

Line Out (left and right)   The sockets used to connect a portastudio to a stereo cassette recorder when mixing on to normal stereo cassette, or to an amplifier for playback over loudspeakers.

MIDI   Musical Instrument Digital Interface. This is how electronic instruments and computers are able to 'talk' to each other.

Mixing   The combining of several audio signals (Chapter 3).

Monitoring   Listening to what you are doing, usually with headphones or loud-speakers. Monitoring means that you can switch between different sound sources or mixes. For example, you may wish to monitor the incoming sound and then switch to the recorded sound 'off tape' to compare the two.

Monmix (Tape Cue)   An additional mixer on a portastudio, this usually consists of four knobs corresponding to the four tape tracks which allow you to listen to a mono version of anything recorded on the tape. This is useful when adding more tracks or punching in (Chapters 1 and 2).

Noise Gate   A useful device which only lets sound through to the recorder when it reaches a predetermined level. This will effectively 'switch off' a MIC when there is nothing to be recorded and therefore eliminates a lot of unwanted background noise (Chapter 14).

Noise Reduction   *see* Dolby and DBX.

Ohms   A measurement of electrical resistance.

Pan   A control which sends a sound to the right, the left, or somewhere in between (Chapters 2 and 3).

Phono   The name given to the input sockets on an amplifier where you connect a record player, also used on other audio equipment.

PPM (peak programme meter)   A type of meter found on mixing consoles and expensive portastudios, it is most likely to consist of a row of little lights (LEDs) and it measures, very rapidly, the peak signal strength rather than the average signal measured by VU meters. It is the most accurate form of meter (Chapter 1).

Punch In (drop in, spot edit)   The process of re-recording a small part of a track while keeping the rest of it.

Record Level   The level or loudness of sound being recorded on to tape. Record levels are displayed by either PPM meters or VU meters, but these should be thought of as a guide. Ears are always the best judge.

Reverb   An effect which gives the illusion of space (for example, a large hall or cavern) to a recording (Chapter 14).

Spot Edit   *see* Punch In.

Sync Track (synchronisation track)   One track on a portastudio which is used to record an electronic 'clock' pulse. This 'clock' is then used to play electronic instruments via a MIDI sequencer. This means they need not be recorded on to the tape. A sync track may also be used to lock one tape machine to another to give more available tracks.

Tape Cue   The controls on a portastudio which enable play-back of the recording of each track of tape. Also see **Monmix**.

Track   One recorded part of a tape: 4-track means that the machine divides the tape into four simultaneous parts and is able to record and replay each one independently (Chapter 1).

Trim (Gain)   An extra volume boost on an input channel. It increases the level for a microphone or electric guitar (Chapter 2).

Voice over   Recording a sung or spoken voice part over a pre-recorded backing.

VU Meter (volume unit)   A type of meter found on mixers and portastudios. It usually has a needle to show the signal level but it measures only the average level of the sound and is not as quick or accurate as a PPM (Chapter 1).

Wow and Flutter   Changes of pitch which occur when there are small changes in the speed of a tape. This can happen when recording and when playing back. Wow refers to slow drifts in pitch which are audible. Flutter refers to very fast changes of pitch heard as distortion.

PART ONE
THE PORTASTUDIO

CHAPTER 1

A QUICK GUIDED TOUR

When a company called TASCAM made their 4-track cassette recorder they called it a 'Portastudio' because it described exactly what a multitrack cassette recorder is: a portable recording studio in a single box.

Nowadays several other companies make multitrack cassette recorders, but the term portastudio has stuck and we shall use it in this book even when we are not referring to TASCAM machines.

There are over thirty different models of portastudio in existence today and although they all look very different, they all work on a similar principle.

Let's take a closer look at the different parts that combine to make a portastudio.

THE TAPE RECORDER

This part of the portastudio looks familiar enough, just like an ordinary cassette recorder you might have at home. It has the familiar controls such as Stop, Play, Record, and Rewind, and a space where you push in the cassette tape.

There will be a Tape Counter and probably a Reset button which sets the tape counter to zero.

There is an invisible difference however. The cassette recorder at home records and plays back in stereo. Stereo simply means there are two tracks, one for your left ear and one for your right ear.

A stereo recording uses half the cassette tape. When Side 1 of the tape has finished you can turn it over and listen to Side 2.

How does the tape record the two sides?

Suppose you had incredible magnetic X-ray vision and could see the music recorded on the tape. Carefully pull a short section of the tape out of the front of the cassette and lay it flat on the table – with your X-ray vision it would look something like this:

SIDE 1 left

right

SIDE 2 right

left

As you can see, the tape is actually divided into four simultaneous bands called Tracks. On a home cassette recorder you listen to only two of these at a time, depending on which side of the tape is being played. The two tracks you are not listening to are recorded on the tape backwards ready for you to turn the cassette over.

On a portastudio, however, you can record on, and listen back to, all four tracks. To prove this, try playing a normal cassette in the portastudio. If you turn all four tracks up you will hear a mixture of music playing forwards and backwards.

Using your X-ray vision on a cassette recorded on a portastudio, you would see it like this:

Track 1

Track 2

Track 3

Track 4

This time all the tracks are recorded in the same direction. Track 4 might be the bass line, track 1 the singer, with a guitar on track 3 and a flute on track 2. Because all the instruments are on their own separate tracks you can choose to play back any combination, and you can decide how loud they should be.

For example, you may not like the singer's recording. No problem! You can turn the track off, or re-record a new vocal track over the one you don't like. If you re-record, then you will still be able to keep the other three tracks containing the bass, guitar and flute.

One word of warning: don't try to turn the tape over to record on the other side! Because the portastudio uses all the tape in one direction you will rub out your recordings starting from the end and working towards the beginning.

Let's take a quick look at the rest of our portastudio.

The Mixer

Look at your portastudio: you will probably be able to see some sliders (called Faders) and several rows of controls. This is the Mixer. The mixer controls the volume of sound during the recording, and when you replay the tape.

The faders set the volume level of each microphone or electric instrument. When the fader is at its lowest position there will be no sound at all. As you push the fader up, the sound will get louder.

There will be more than one fader so you can record or play back more than one instrument at a time, and there will be a Master Fader which controls all the others. You could use this to fade out all the instruments at the end of a song.

Some of the other controls will change the tone quality of a sound, or select which of the four tracks for a sound to be recorded.

The Meters

Look for the set of meters, probably four, which show the strength of the sound.

There are two types of meter found on portastudio mixers. Some meters use a moving needle to show the level of the sound. Others use a row of little lights (called Light Emitting Diodes or LEDs for short). As the sound gets louder, more of them light up.

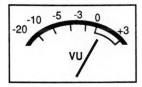

VU meter showing the
strength of the sound
just entering into 'the red'

either:
or:

left	right		aux	
trk 1	2	3	4	
▓	▓	▓	▓	+5
▓	▓	▓	▓	+3
▓	▓	▓	▓	+1
▓	▓	▓	▓	0
▯	▯	▯	▯	-1
▯	▯	▯	▯	-3
▯	▯	▯	▯	-5
▯	▯	▯	▯	-7
▯	▯	▯	▯	-10
▯	▯	▯	▯	-15
▯	▯	▯	▯	-20
▯	▯	▯	▯	

*4 LED type meters. The lights below the
0 line are usually orange or green.
Those above are red*

The meters will show the levels of each individual tape track, or the stereo sound from the mixer. There will be a switch to select the options.

Both types of meter have a scale that starts around −20 and ends at about +5. The part of the scale from 0 to +5 will be shown in red. Always aim to record an instrument so that the meters just go 'into the red' (past the 0 mark), but you need to be a little careful.

Most instruments, especially acoustic ones and voices, vary enormously during a performance and you will need to check the levels during rehearsal. Try to find the loudest part of the music and set the faders so that the meters show about +2. If possible, leave the faders at this level throughout the recording.

Meters are only a guide to the level of recording. The basic rule is to use your ears. If it sounds distorted, they're set too high.

Noise Reduction

There are two main types of Noise Reduction system: Dolby which is also used on domestic equipment, and DBX. The portastudio will have a single noise reduction switch to switch it on or off.

Let's look at what the noise reduction does. Try playing a brand new unrecorded cassette on your portastudio or normal cassette player with the noise reduction switch off. If you turn the volume control up you will hear a hiss from the tape.

All tapes have this hiss on them, even the very good quality ones, although the problem is worse on cheaper tapes, of course. Worse still, because you may be listening to all four tracks on a portastudio, rather than two on an ordinary cassette deck you will hear twice the amount of tape hiss.

Obviously this could become very annoying, especially when recording a quiet instrument such as a vibraphone. The noise reduction system is used to get rid of this tape hiss.

Unfortunately noise reduction will not get rid of any other noise, such as hiss and crackle from a guitar amp, a noisy instrument lead, or the class next door. (If any of these are problems, Chapter 15, 'In the Classroom', has some advice.) Also, noise reduction will only work if you use it while recording. If you have a recorded tape with lots of hiss on it, bad luck!

There are occasions when you may not wish to use noise reduction. It can sometimes make the sound seem duller, for example, and that is the reason most machines provide an off switch. Before you start recording, remember to check if it's on or off!

The Monitor Mixer

Most portastudios don't have just one mixer, but two. Sometimes called Monmix or Tape Cue, this simple monitor mixer is included in the larger machines to make it easier to record new material while listening to the play-back of previously recorded tracks. The monitor mixer will allow you to hear a combination of the sound already recorded on the tape with the sound you are about to record. It usually consists of four volume controls, one for each track of tape, and is especially useful if you wish to re-record a small section of a track, perhaps a few bars where you made a mistake. Using the monitor mixer you can listen to the track containing the mistake while you play along with it, checking that you are in time and in tune. You will then be able to hear the exact point at which to re-record.

THE PITCH CONTROL

This changes the pitch of the recording by changing the speed of the tape. Slow the tape down and you lower the pitch, speed the tape up and you raise the pitch. But why would you want to? Here are two possible reasons:

1 Suppose you've recorded a brilliant performance of a guitar on one track. You go to record an acoustic piano but find that although 'in tune with itself', the guitar was not tuned to the same pitch as the piano – let's say it was tuned flat. You could retune the guitar and re-record the track, but the first guitar recording is so brilliant you doubt if it can be repeated! The solution is to use the pitch control to speed up the tape slightly until the recorded guitar is at the same pitch as the piano. When you've recorded the piano you can return the tape to its original speed and pitch.

2 Your singer may be having trouble reaching the high notes of the music you are recording and it therefore sounds out of tune. You may find it helps the singer if you drop the pitch of the other tracks by a semitone or two while recording. Of course, this will slow the tempo down a little, but that will not usually matter. On replaying the tape or recording another instrument, you can return the pitch and tempo to the original setting and the singer will hit the top notes with ease!

CHAPTER 2

LET'S RECORD – MAKING A JINGLE

Let's record some music on to the portastudio!

First we need something to record. Using an electronic keyboard, let's make up a short piece of music to use on an answer-phone. On top of the music we'll use a microphone to record a Voice-over asking callers to leave their name and number. Here's the plan for the answer-phone jingle written on a Tracksheet:

RECORDING TRACKSHEET

TITLE: answer-phone jingle

Track 1	Music >>>>>>>>>>>>>>>>>>>>>>>>>>>>>>>>>>
Track 2	Spoken Voice >>>>>>>>>>
Track 3	(blank)
Track 4	(blank)

This is what you will need:

an electronic keyboard with a suitable lead to plug it into the portastudio

a microphone

a chrome tape (if you have only an ordinary tape, use that for now, but buy a chrome tape because portastudios work much better with them)

headphones to listen to the recording (or you could plug the portastudio into your hi-fi, or even an instrument amp. Making these connections is explained in Chapter 15.)

Make up a short piece of music on the electronic keyboard. It shouldn't last more than 25 seconds because that's probably the maximum time the answer-phone will allow.

Either try this idea, or make up your own music.

Find a rhythm you like on the keyboard. Switch on the one-fingered automatic chords, and play the following notes on the lowest part of the keyboard:

F   A   F   D

Here's where they are on the keyboard:

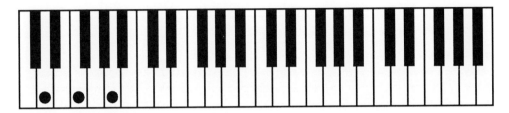

C D E F G A B C D E F G A B C D E F G A B C D E F G A B

and this is how the notes are written in music notation:

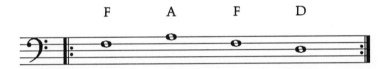

You may be happy to record the chords on their own, or you could make up a tune to play with them. When you are ready, record your keyboard music on to track 1 of the tape. Here's how . . .

SET UP THE PORTASTUDIO

Switch the portastudio on, put the tape in. Rewind it to the beginning. Set the Tape Counter to zero.

Plug in the headphones (unless you have your portastudio plugged into the hi-fi or an amplifier). Find the headphones' volume control and turn it up about half-way.

PLUG IN THE KEYBOARD

Look for the first Input socket for track 1 and connect the keyboard into it. If there is a choice between MIC and LINE input sockets, use the line for electronic instruments.

SET THE MIXER CONTROLS

Find the first channel of the mixer. It will probably look something like this:

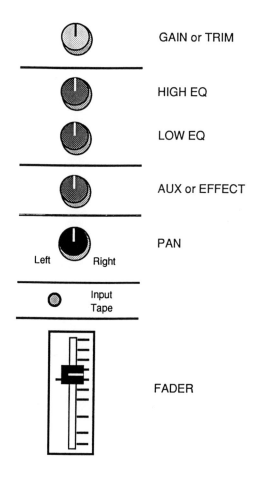

Your portastudio may not have all these controls, and they may not be laid out like this. Don't worry!

The mixer needs the answers to these questions:

Question
Is channel 1 being used to record something, or play back the tape?

Answer
Record something.

What to do
The mixer channel will have a switch to select either the tape replay or the instrument being recorded. Set the switch to the INPUT/LINE setting.

Question
Are you recording through a
microphone, or directly, using an
electronic instrument?

Answer
An electronic instrument.

What to do
Some portastudios have separate input
sockets for microphones (MIC) and
electronic instruments (LINE).
Otherwise, look for a switch marked
MIC/LINE, or try the GAIN/TRIM
control. Use the LINE setting.

Question
What do you want the meters to
show?

Answer
The level of the keyboard to be
recorded.

What to do
Find a switch to tell the four meters
to show each individual track of tape.
Look for the TAPE, TRK, or RECORDER
setting.

Question
Which tape track do you want to
record on to?

Answer
Let's record on track 1.

What to do
Find the switches that select the
recording track. Look for track 1 and
set it to Left:

May look like this

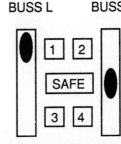

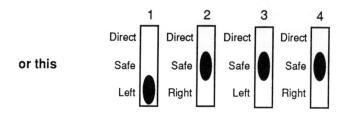

or this

This tells tape track 1 to record everything directed to the left BUSS (route). The sound is directed by the PAN control . . .

Now find the PAN control on channel 1 and turn this all the way to the left.

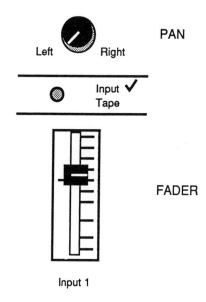

Think of the PAN control as a 'traffic cop' directing the sound traffic. Here are two examples:

1 the Pan control sends all the sound to the left Buss to be recorded on either track 1 or 3.

2 the Pan control sends some of the sound to the left Buss, and the rest to the right Buss, so it could be recorded on any of the four tracks.

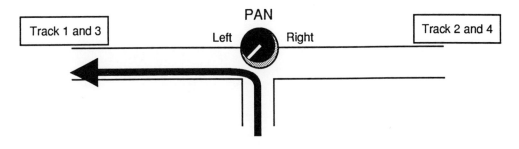

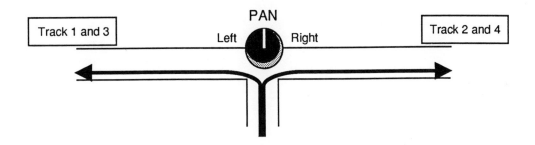

Question
How loud do you want to record the instrument?

Answer
Quite loud (you can always turn it down later if you need to).

What to do
Find the MASTER FADER and raise this about three-quarters of the way. Play the keyboard and move the fader up until meter 1 shows a signal.
You may need to press RECORD and PAUSE to make the meter work.

Press RECORD, and play the keyboard. When you have finished, rewind the tape, set the track 1 Record Select switch to Safe, and get ready to listen to the recording.

Recording Tracksheet

Track 1   keyboard
Track 2   _____
Track 3   _____
Track 4   _____

PLAY-BACK

At this stage, the best way to check the recording is to use the MONITOR MIXER (MONMIX). You will need to tell the headphones to play back the Monmix – look for the switch. Also turn all the Monmix volume controls up about half-way.

When you listen to the music, make up a short spoken message to record on the next track. The message should start after the music begins and end a little before the music ends, so you will need to practise it. When you are ready, set up the portastudio to record on track 2. Here's how . . .

RECORDING THE VOICE ON TRACK 2

Unplug the keyboard from Input 1, replace it with the microphone.

Once again the mixer needs the answers to these questions:

Question
Is channel 1 being used to record something, or play back the tape?

Answer
Record something.

What to do
Set the switch to INPUT/MIC.

Question
Are you recording through a microphone, or directly on an electronic instrument?

Answer
Microphone.

What to do
This time use either the separate input socket for microphones (MIC), look for a switch marked MIC/LINE and set it to MIC, or turn the GAIN/TRIM control to the MIC position.

GAIN or TRIM

Mic
Line

Line   Mic

The most suitable setting will be somewhere within this range, depending on the sensitivity of the microphone

Question
What do you want the meters to show?

Answer
The level of the microphone being recorded.

What to do
Nothing . . . you have already set this switch to show the four tape tracks.

Question
Which tape track do you want to record on to?

Answer
Track 2 this time.

What to do
Find the switches that select the recording track. Look for track 2 and set it to Right.

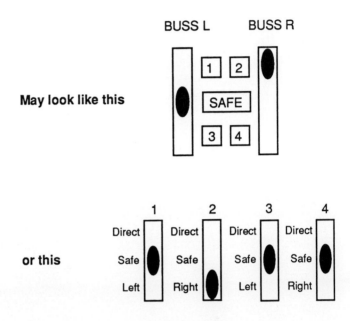

May look like this

or this

This tells tape track 2 to record everything directed to the right BUSS.

Now find the PAN control on channel 1 and turn this all the way to the right.

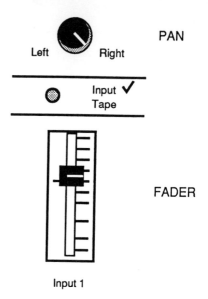

Input 1

Question	*Answer*
How loud do you want to record the voice?	Quite loud.
	What to do
	Speak into the microphone and move the fader up until meter 2 shows a signal.
	You may need to press RECORD and PAUSE to make the meter work.

Press RECORD, and record the voice-over. When you have finished, rewind the tape, set the track 2 RECORD SELECT switch to SAFE, and listen to the recording of both tracks.

Recording Tracksheet

Track 1   keyboard
Track 2   voice
Track 3
Track 4

CHAPTER 3

LET'S MIX – MIXING THE JINGLE

Now we have recorded our answer-phone jingle, let's mix it!

Mixing means making your recording sound as good as possible by adjusting the level and tone quality of each track, and cutting out any parts you decide not to use.

You will probably want to record your mix on to a stereo cassette. If so, connect your portastudio to a stereo cassette recorder like this:

Playback...   ...Record

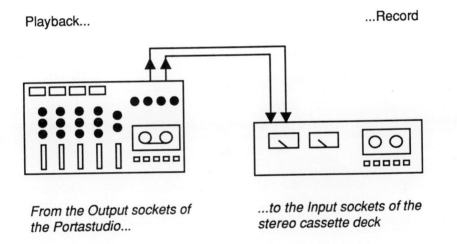

From the Output sockets of   ...to the Input sockets of the
the Portastudio...   stereo cassette deck

To mix, first put the tape into the portastudio. Rewind it to the beginning. Set the TAPE COUNTER to zero.

This time, when you play back the tape, don't listen to it on the MONMIX. Instead, play back the tape through the main mixer – the faders you used to record. You can then use the faders to control the volume, and the EQ (equalisation) controls to change the tone quality. When mixing, the PAN controls send the sound to the left and right speakers.

Now set the headphones to play back the sound from the mixer. Try the REMIX setting.

The mixer needs the answers to these questions:

Question	Answer
Is the mixer being used to record something, or play back the tape?	Play back the tape.

What to do
Find the switches that tell channels
1 and 2 to play back the tape.

Question
What do you want the meters to
show?

Answer
The level of the mixed sound.

What to do
Find the switch to tell the meters to
show the stereo output from the
mixer.

Play the tape. The channel 1 fader will control the sound of the keyboard, the
channel 2 fader the sound of the voice, and the master fader the overall level.
  If your portastudio has EQ controls, try using them to change the tone quality.
  If your portastudio has EQ controls on each input channel, they will be above or
to one side of the fader and may be small sliders, or knobs that rotate.

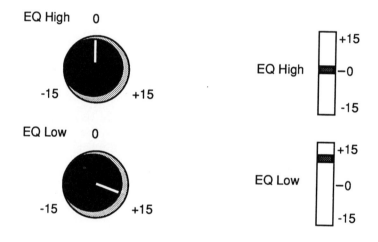

Rotating variety of EQ controls   *Slider EQ controls*

In either case there will be a control for the high (treble) sound and another for the
low (bass). Look for the high (treble) control. When the control is at the centre
position the sound is exactly as it was when it entered the portastudio. Moving
the control in one direction will increase the high frequencies and make the sound
brighter. Move the control in the other direction and the high frequencies will be
filtered out giving the sound a duller feel. Try the low (bass) control now. If you
move the low frequency control as shown in the diagram, the bass will get louder.
Move the controls the other way and the bass will be filtered out. Set the EQ
controls on each track to get the best sound.
  Now set the levels for each track. When the voice starts, you might want the

music to get quieter so that the voice stands out. After the voice has finished, the music can increase in volume again. Use the tape counter to work out when to lower the fader to make the music quieter, and when to raise it at the end. You should write all the timings and settings down on the tracksheet.

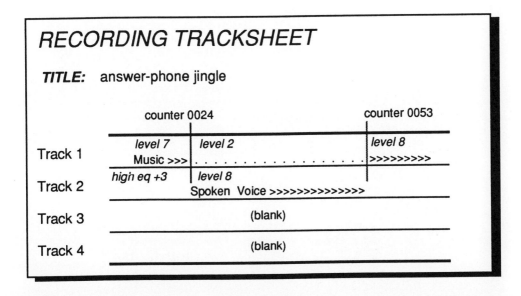

Try using the PAN control to move the sound between the speakers. When you are ready, record your mix on to the stereo cassette tape.

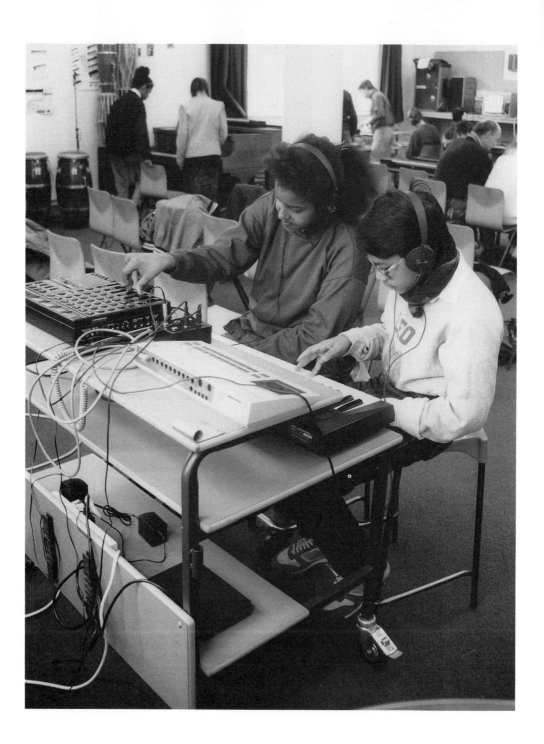

PART TWO
COMPOSING

COMPOSITION PROJECTS

The projects in the following chapters range in complexity from 'Using Chords', which assumes little or no previous knowledge or technical skill to 'Music from Africa', which might be used as a starting point by pupils with experience of harmonic and rhythmic structures. Each project is intended as a guide to show how the portastudio might be used to help pupils compose. They are not intended to be self-contained 'worksheets' and teachers will almost certainly wish to adapt them to suit their particular situation.

The ideas are not exclusive to the project in which they appear – pupils 'making an advert' may decide, for example, to use a rap, or some material based on the 'Music from Africa' chapter.

Most importantly, pupils should always be encouraged to develop their own musical ideas instead of using the examples included in this chapter exclusively.

Each chapter includes ideas for follow-up work, or suggestions on extending and developing the project. Finally, each project ends with examples of specific criteria for assessing the pupils' composing work.

For all the composition projects, general assessment criteria might include consideration of:

1   The process of composition:
    How has the pupil contributed to the group?
    Which parts of the composition have been developed by the pupil independently?
    Has the pupil kept working notes including record sheets and track sheets?
    Teachers may find the 'Composition Diary' record sheet in Chapter 12 a useful way of jotting down short comments and notes about a pupil's work throughout a project. This lesson-by-lesson diary will help pupils and teachers keep track of the composition, agree on short-term aims (i.e. the next stage) and contribute to the teacher's final assessment.

2   The finished composition:
    Communication to the listener.
    Musical ideas: relevance to the project brief.
    Development of the musical material.
    Imaginative use of the available resources.
    Skill in composing for the selected resources.

This project is for pupils who have some experience, however limited, of using chords to make music. It uses a simple 12-bar blues chord sequence in C, over which pupils may record improvised melody lines. Once the pupils are familiar with the chords, they may wish to use them as the basis for a song.

THE BASS LINE

Let's start with a bass line which you could play on a xylophone or a keyboard. This bass line uses three notes: C, F, and G. The picture shows where these notes are; find them on your xylophone or keyboard.

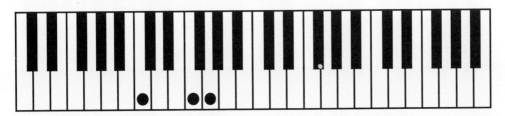

CDEFGABCDEFGABCDEFGABCDEFGAB

Play the notes in this order to make the bass line;
C C C C / C C C C / C C C C / C C C C / F F F F / F F F F / C C C C / C C C C /
G G G G / F F F F / C C C C / C C C C
You may find it easier to count like this:

C	16 times (4×4)
F	8 times (2×4)
C	8 times (2×4)
G	4 times (1×4)
F	4 times (1×4)
C	8 times (2×4)

You will need to play all the notes to a regular pulse with no gaps in between. Try playing with a metronome or a drum machine. When you get to the end, start at the beginning again. When you can repeat the whole bass line several times without any mistakes, record it on to track 1 of the portastudio.

Recording Tracksheet

Track 1   ░░░░░   bass line   ░░░░░
Track 2   _____
Track 3   _____
Track 4   _____

THE CHORDS

When you are happy with the recording of your bass line, you can try some chords that will fit with it.

Playing these notes together will make a C chord: **C   E   G**
Here's where they are on the keyboard

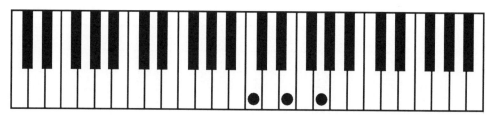

C D E F G A B C D E F G A B C D E F G A B C D E F G A B

The following notes played together make an F chord: **F   A   C**
Here's where they are on the keyboard

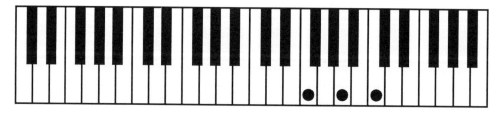

C D E F G A B C D E F G A B C D E F G A B C D E F G A B

These notes played together make a G chord: **G   B   D**
Here's where they are on the keyboard

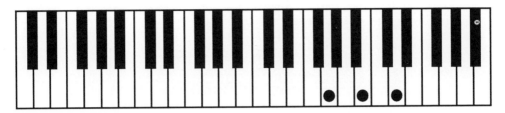

C D E F G A B C D E F G A B C D E F G A B C D E F G A B

Now try playing the chords with the bass line you've recorded on track 1. If you are using a xylophone play one or two of the notes in the chord. If you are playing a keyboard you could try all three.

The basic idea is to play the C Chord when the bass line is C, the F chord when the bass line is F, and the G chord when the bass line is G.

You could either play one chord for each note in the bass line, or play one chord to last through four bass line notes like this:

listen to the Bass Line *(Track 1)*	C C C C	C C C C	C C C C	C C C C	F F F F	F F F F
try playing *these chords:*	G E C	G E C	G E C	G E C	C A F	C A F

listen to the Bass Line *(Track 1)*	C C C C	C C C C	G G G G	F F F F	C C C C	C C C C
try playing *these chords:*	G E C	G E C	D B G	C A F	G E C	G E C

Practise playing the chords to the bass line. Don't forget to change chord when the note in the bass line changes! When you are ready record the chords on to track 2.

```
┌─────────────────────────────────────────────────┐
│                                                   │
│     Recording Tracksheet                          │
│                                                   │
│     Track 1  ░░░░░░  bass line  ░░░░░░             │
│     Track 2  ░░░░░   chords   ░░░░░░               │
│     Track 3  ──────────────────────────           │
│     Track 4  ──────────────────────────           │
│                                                   │
└─────────────────────────────────────────────────┘
```

The Tune

Look at the notes you used to make up the C chord. They are C, E and G. Start by using these notes one at a time to make your tune. Here are two starting suggestions:

No. 1

listen to the Bass Line (Track 1)	C C C C	C C C C	C C C C	C C C C	F F F F	F F F F
and the chords (Track 2)	G E C	G E C	G E C	G E C	C A F	C A F

try making a tune: C C E G   C C E G   ....

No. 2

listen to the Bass Line (Track 1)	C C C C	C C C C	C C C C	C C C C	F F F F	F F F F
and the chords (Track 2)	G E C	G E C	G E C	G E C	C A F	C A F

try making a tune: CEG ▬▬ CEG ▬▬ ....

When the chord changes to F, then use the notes of the F chord to make the tune.

Play back the bass line and the chords (on tracks 1 and 2), and try making the tune fit. When it begins to sound all right, record your tune on to track 3.

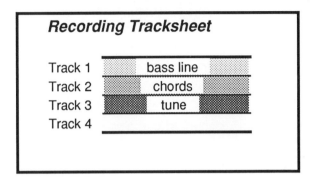

FOLLOW-UP WORK

• Chords   Obviously this is a very basic introduction to chords and melody. Many pupils will discover chords other than the basic major triads (e.g. C, E, G) together with key relationships for themselves through practical work.

Others will need help from the teacher. A starting-point might be to explain to pupils that any note may be used as the bottom, middle or top note of a triad and to suggest they find as many chords as they can using a keyboard or tuned percussion instrument.

The basic structure is a 12-bar blues, and pupils may wish to explore this style of music further, introducing the idea of 'blue notes', seventh chords, and improvisation.

• Pupils may wish to explore a range of rhythmic patterns when composing a tune. The use of dotted rhythms and tied notes could be introduced at this stage.

• Some pupils may wish to add a voice part. This could be recorded on track 4.

ASSESSMENT

Invention of melodic lines:
shape of each phrase, evidence of development in the melodic line, consistency of style, rhythmic invention, does the melody work well with the chords?
Selection of appropriate instruments and voices. Choice of sounds from an electronic keyboard.

And if pupils explore further:
Development of chords and chord sequences using pupils' own chords.
Development of the bass line: shape of each phrase, selection of notes other than the root of each chord, variety of rhythm, consistency of style.
Imaginative use of melodic instruments and voice: do the instruments/voices complement each other?

This project should help pupils to make a song within the tradition of any popular culture, for example hip-hop, ballad, Indian film songs, Bhangra.

Pupils will probably work most productively in small groups with different members contributing ideas for discussion as well as bringing their individual skills to the project. Pupils should be encouraged to record their ideas on to one of the portastudio tracks from the start so that different versions can be compared, and new material worked out while listening to the initial recording.

An alternative to group work would be for a pupil to build up the song by recording each part, track by track, either playing all the material individually, or by working out parts for other pupils with specific instrumental skills to play, just like 'session musicians' in the recording industry.

Cross-curricular links
Where possible this project might support language work in either English, another school-taught language, or the mother tongue of pupils who are learning English as a second language.

Pupils might be encouraged to write their own words and consider the type of words and structure suitable for being set to music. Rhyme and meter will need to be considered.

BUILDING A SONG

Most popular songs have some or all of the following parts:

Vocals
The words (lyrics) are usually sung by a lead singer who is sometimes accompanied by backing singers.

The drum beat
This might be played on a drum kit, tablas, congas, an electronic drum machine, or a combination of them all.

Chords
These could be played on a keyboard, a guitar, a xylophone, or a combination of these instruments.

The bass line

This may be played on a bass guitar, the low end of a keyboard, or a low instrument such as a cello or a tenor saxophone.

There are no rules about how a song is put together. Some people prefer to start with the drum, bass or chords. This chapter shows how to start a song with the vocal part.

THE WORDS AND THE TUNE

You can find some suitable words, such as a poem, or make up some of your own. Some people find it easier to make up a tune and then find some words to fit it. Others prefer to write the lyrics first and let the music follow the flow of the words.

In either case you need to decide what the song is about, what you want it to say. For example, you might decide to write a song about falling in (or out of) love. Love is a popular subject for songwriters, and probably features in at least half the songs ever written! Here is a possible first line for a song about a relationship:

We were happy from the start . . .

Let's try and work out a tune for this line. We have to decide the type of music to use that will reflect the mood of the words. If we felt, for example, that the song was going to be about breaking up, we might decide to make the music slow and sad in the style of a ballad.

Try singing the line, or try playing some notes on a keyboard that fit to the words. You may find it helpful to follow a musical shape like this:

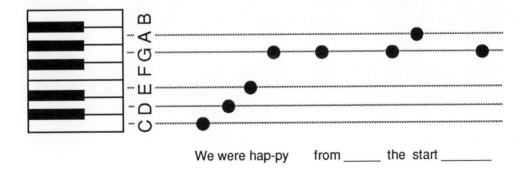

We were hap-py   from _____ the start _____

Once you have the first line worked out, try making up the second. The tune might continue by repeating the same pattern. This has the advantage of letting your audience hear it twice, more chance they will remember it!

Or try turning the shape backwards: (starting at the end and singing the notes back to the beginning)

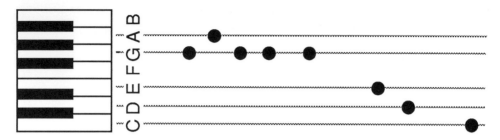

Now for the second line of words: if you think the two lines should rhyme then you need to find a word that rhymes with 'start'. How about 'heart'?

We were happy from the start,
And you la la la my heart . . .

Yes, the line isn't finished yet, but you don't need to finish the lyrics completely at this stage. Just sing 'la' and fill the words in later!

For the third line of music try using the first line again, but change it slightly at the end. For example, our tune ended by going down a little on the last note. Try going up a little instead.

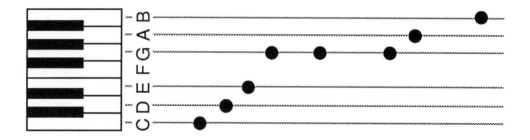

Try recording the first part of your song on to track 1 of the portastudio. If you think your song will eventually use drums or percussion you will find it helps to record a metronome on another track. This is called a 'click track' and is often used in studio recordings. If you sing to this it will help you keep in time and make further recordings such as the chords and bass line much easier. If you think you will use a drum machine, then you should record it at this point because the machine will not be able to follow you if you speed up or slow down. Drum machines always set the speed of the song. If you are using the type of drum machine which lets you set the speed (tempo), then you can record a guide version of the drum track now and work out the final version later.

You may like to record several versions, one after the other. Play them all to the group, or your friends, and choose the best one. You can then wipe off all the recordings you don't want.

Recording Tracksheet

Track 1 ▓▓▓ tune ▓▓▓
Track 2 _____
Track 3 _____
Track 4 _____

THE DRUM BEAT

You can make the drum track with acoustic percussion such as a drum kit, with a drum machine, or with the rhythm section of an electronic keyboard. Don't be surprised if you can't make the drum part fit to the vocal track. You will probably need to re-record your tune with the drum beat. This is because the drummer's job is to set the speed and keep time. Usually all the other musicians follow the drum part.

If there are no drummers to help you, then the best advice on making drum beats is to keep them simple. You can always add more later, drum rolls for example. You could start with a bass drum and snare, or a bass drum and high hat cymbal to make the speed clear. Try playing the bass drum on the strong words of the lyrics if you are not sure where to begin!

Recording Tracksheet

Track 1 ░░░ tune ░░░
Track 2 ▨▨▨ drums ▨▨▨
Track 3 _____
Track 4 _____

THE CHORDS

Choose the instruments you want to use to make the chord track. If you are using a synthesiser or electronic keyboard you will need to choose one or more of the sounds.

Play the tape and try out some chords with the tune. If you don't know where to begin, try making a chord around the notes in the tune like this:

Find the strong words in the song:

In the example the strong words could be 'happy' and 'start'. In the case of the word 'happy' the strong bit is the first part of the word, 'ha'.

We were **happy** from the **start**

Check what notes are used on the strong words.

A tune note can be the bottom, middle, or top of a three-note chord. Take the note E we used for the first strong word ('**ha**ppy') in our opening line. If we make this the top note of a chord then we can try two other notes underneath. Try these possibilities:

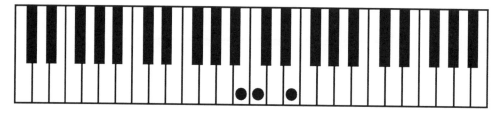

C D E F G A B C D E F G A B C D E F G A B C D E F G A B

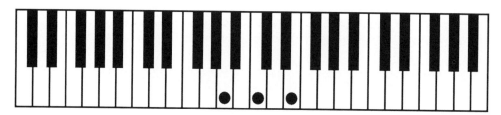

C D E F G A B C D E F G A B C D E F G A B C D E F G A B

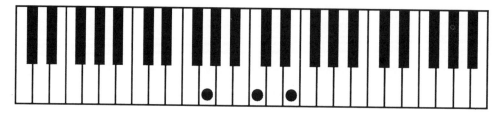

C D E F G A B C D E F G A B C D E F G A B C D E F G A B

Try making chords on all the strong words in the lyrics, then keep playing the chord until the next strong word. You can decide if they sound good when you play them with the vocal line. When you have made a series of chords, record them on track 3 of the tape.

```
┌─────────────────────────────────────────────────┐
│  ┌───────────────────────────────────────────┐  │
│  │  Recording Tracksheet                     │  │
│  │                                           │  │
│  │  Track 1  ░░░░░░░░  tune  ░░░░░░░░         │  │
│  │  Track 2  ░░░░░░░░  drums  ░░░░░░░░        │  │
│  │  Track 3  ░░░░░░░░  chords  ░░░░░░░░       │  │
│  │  Track 4  ───────────────────────────     │  │
│  │                                           │  │
│  └───────────────────────────────────────────┘  │
└─────────────────────────────────────────────────┘
```

THE BASS LINE

If you don't know where to begin then find the lowest note of each chord and play that. (If you are not happy with some of your bass notes, try the middle note in the chord.) When you can play this basic bass line you can then try varying the notes. Bass players often add additional notes between the main 'strong' ones.

When you are happy with your bass line, record it on to the remaining track.

```
┌─────────────────────────────────────────────────┐
│  ┌───────────────────────────────────────────┐  │
│  │  Recording Tracksheet                     │  │
│  │                                           │  │
│  │  Track 1  ░░░░░░░░  tune  ░░░░░░░░         │  │
│  │  Track 2  ░░░░░░░░  drums  ░░░░░░░░        │  │
│  │  Track 3  ░░░░░░░░  chords  ░░░░░░░░       │  │
│  │  Track 4  ░░░░░░░░  bass  ░░░░░░░░         │  │
│  │                                           │  │
│  └───────────────────────────────────────────┘  │
└─────────────────────────────────────────────────┘
```

Follow-up work

Listen to some songs on the radio or cassette and work out the structure.

For example, find out the shape of the tune and how it varies. Is there a verse/chorus structure? Do the words rhyme and if so, where? Are there changes in the drum pattern, or the instruments that are used? If so, where do these changes occur?

Assessment

Development and shape of melody.

Appropriate combination of melody and lyrics.

Inventiveness and use of other voice parts, additional instrumental parts.

Choice of chords and rhythm.

The overall form and structure of the song.

Appropriate style.

CHAPTER 6

THE INDIAN INFLUENCE

In the West there is a long history of borrowing musical ideas from other cultures and using them within the traditions of Western classical and popular music. Since the advent of radio and recording there has been a much greater exchange of musical ideas around the world. An example of this is found in Bhangra, a type of Indian popular music influenced by Indian and Western music. This project is designed to introduce pupils to some aspects of Indian music. It is, however, no substitute for the real thing although it might lead on to an exploration and greater understanding of authentic Indian music.

Cross-curricular links
Much Indian music is tied to dance and religion. There may be opportunities to explore both of these aspects within Dance, R.E., History, and Geography departments.

THE ESSENTIALS

Starting with the Beat
Indian musicians use different instruments to make a beat depending on the type of music being played. You could use percussion instruments such as tablas, congas, or a drum kit. You could use a drum machine but you will need one that you can play live, or programme the dynamics (loud and soft).

Start by recording a steady drum beat on to track 1. It should be played at a speed of about 160 beats per minute. If you don't know how fast this is, ask your teacher to show you.

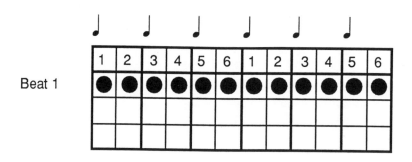

```
┌──────────────────────────────────────┐
│                                        │
│      Recording Tracksheet              │
│                                        │
│      Track 1  ▒▒▒▒ steady beat ▒▒▒▒    │
│      Track 2  ─────────────────────    │
│      Track 3  ─────────────────────    │
│      Track 4  ─────────────────────    │
│                                        │
└──────────────────────────────────────┘
```

On track 2 we need to record some strong accented beats. Count in sixes to the click track and try playing another drum on every 2nd and 3rd beat.

A third drum might play every 6th beat.

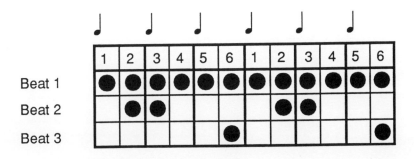

```
┌──────────────────────────────────────┐
│                                        │
│      Recording Tracksheet              │
│                                        │
│      Track 1  ▒▒▒▒ steady beat ▒▒▒▒    │
│      Track 2  ▨▨ accented beats ▨▨     │
│      Track 3  ─────────────────────    │
│      Track 4  ─────────────────────    │
│                                        │
└──────────────────────────────────────┘
```

The melody line

One of the distinctive aspects of Indian music is the notes it uses. Here are the notes of three Indian 'scales' or 'ragas'. Try playing them up and down and listen to the effect:

1st Raga notes

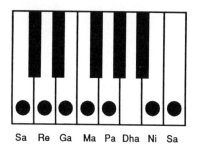

Sa Re Ga Ma Pa Dha Ni Sa

Sa, Re, Ga, Ma, Pa, Ni
(C, D, E, F, G, B)

2nd Raga notes

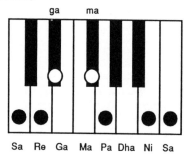

Sa Re Ga Ma Pa Dha Ni Sa

Sa, Re, ga, ma, Pa, Ni
(C, D, E flat, F sharp, G, B)

3rd Raga notes

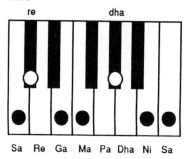

Sa Re Ga Ma Pa Dha Ni Sa

Sa, re, Ga, Ma, dha, Ni
(C, D flat, E, F, A flat, B)

Now try improvising a melody line using only the notes of one of these scales. Indian musicians don't just play the notes up and down in order, they make the tune twist and turn, and use their skill to vary the way they play the notes. Practise using different patterns of notes, different speeds and rhythms, and loud and soft phrases. When you are ready record your melody on to track 3.

```
┌──────────────────────────────────────────────┐
│                                                │
│   Recording Tracksheet                         │
│                                                │
│   Track 1  ┌────────────────────────┐          │
│            │      steady beat        │          │
│   Track 2  │ ▨▨▨ accented beats ▨▨▨ │          │
│   Track 3  │ ⋰⋰⋱   melody   ⋰⋱⋰⋱ │          │
│   Track 4  └────────────────────────┘          │
│                                                │
└──────────────────────────────────────────────┘
```

The Drone

A drone is one note, usually low-pitched, which plays throughout the piece. A lot of music all over the world uses a drone instead of a bass line.

The drone in this piece could be the lowest note of the scale you are using, and you need to choose an instrument that can keep the note going for as long as possible. You could use a string instrument, such as a cello, or a note held down on an electric organ, or you could even try singing it if you have a lot of breath! Record the drone on track 4.

```
┌──────────────────────────────────────────────┐
│                                                │
│   Recording Tracksheet                         │
│                                                │
│   Track 1  ┌────────────────────────┐          │
│            │      steady beat        │          │
│   Track 2  │ ▨▨▨ accented beats ▨▨▨ │          │
│   Track 3  │ ⋰⋰⋱   melody   ⋰⋱⋰⋱ │          │
│   Track 4  │ ∧∧∧∧∧   drone   ∧∧∧∧∧ │          │
│            └────────────────────────┘          │
│                                                │
└──────────────────────────────────────────────┘
```

Follow-up work

● Pupils may wish to use more extended rhythms than those given in this chapter. Using groups of 16 beats instead of the groups of 6 will give more opportunity for subdivision. For example, a 16-beat group might be divided into 4 + 4 + 3 + 3 + 2.

● Pupils may also be interested in exploring further the range of 'scale systems' found in Indian music. This might lead to an exploration of pentatonic scales found in folk music from around the world, as well as modes.

● Decoration or ornamentation is important in the melodic development of Indian music and pupils may be interested in exploring this. You may wish to make comparisons with the ornamentation used in Western music of different periods.

Assessment

Imaginative use of note patterns, rhythms and dynamics to make the melody.

Development and structure of the melody line: overall shape, ornamentation and variation of basic note patterns, unity of style. Imaginative use of resources: use of appropriate instruments or voices, selection of sounds from electronic keyboards. Inventiveness of rhythmic patterns.

CHAPTER 7
MAKING AN ADVERT

The object of this project is for pupils to produce a short piece of music of agreed duration, for a specific purpose, within a given time limit.

Cross-curricular links
This project closely follows the way adverts are produced in the industry and there may be an opportunity for links with Media Studies, and Business Studies. Many adverts are aimed at a target audience and will be of relevance to Home Economics departments. The English department may be able to support the lyric writing together with the spoken text and the Art department may be able to relate the use of music to create a mood with the use of visual images in the media.

RADIO ADVERTS

A lot of radio adverts are made by small production companies, or by people already working for commercial radio stations. A composer will be used if original music is required. A lot of music for adverts is composed straight on to tape.

There are several ways to put an advert together. You will probably need a spoken message called a 'voice-over', together with a short piece of music. There may be a sung vocal line and you may need to record some background sound or use sound effects.

First of all you need to know what it is you are advertising. The client will tell you what the product is and the length of time booked for the advert on the radio. These are some of the questions you will need to ask before composing your advert.

1 What are you advertising?
2 Who is the advert aimed at?
  Adverts have a 'target audience', perhaps wealthy people, poor people, kids, women, etc. This will affect the type of music you make.
3 How long can it last?
  Adverts have very strict time limits because it costs a lot of money to buy 'airtime'. Time is usually sold in 15-second slots.
4 What resources, such as instruments, are available?
  A production company would need to set a budget, so you might have to do without a full orchestra and use a synthesiser instead!
5 When does it have to be finished?
  Often the airtime is booked before the advert has been made and the composer will have to work to a deadline.

You may find an Advert Production Sheet helpful in your planning:

ADVERT PRODUCTION SHEET

Length of advert in seconds: 20 secs ___ 30 secs ___ 45 secs ___ 60 secs ___

What is the product to be advertised? _____

Who will the advert be aimed at? _____

What style of music would be suitable? _____

What instruments do you wish to use?

Is there a 'voice-over'? Yes ____ No ____

The spoken words are:

The advert must be finished by: _____

This advert was created and produced by: _____

_____

Now that you have decided what sort of advert you are going to make, you will probably find it a good idea to plan the advert on a tracksheet. This will help you decide exactly when the voice has to speak, or when the effects have to happen. Here is an example of a rough sketch for an advert:

	15 secs	30 secs	45 secs	1 min
Track 1	*electronic keyboard* — — — — — — — + — — — — — — — + — — — — — —
Track 2		*vocals (sung)* — —		*vocals (sung)* — —
Track 3			*spoken message* —	
Track 4				

In this example the advert starts with some chords on an electronic keyboard, so this would need to be recorded first on track 1:

Recording Tracksheet

Track 1   keyboard
Track 2 _____
Track 3 _____
Track 4 _____

Next, the singers could be recorded on track 2:

Recording Tracksheet

Track 1   keyboard
Track 2   singers
Track 3 _____
Track 4 _____

Finally, the spoken message could be recorded on track 3:

Recording Tracksheet

Track 1   keyboard
Track 2   singers
Track 3   message
Track 4 _____

When you play back the recording, you will need to adjust the loudness of each track in order to get the best result. For example, you may need to lower the keyboard sound on track 1 during the spoken message on track 3. When the message is over, you can turn the volume of the keyboard up again.

Follow-up work
Let the pupils listen to some radio adverts and invite critical comment. What type of music has been used on the advert, and why? What instruments are playing, what mood has been created, and how does the particular music help create a mood? (Is it tempo, meter, style, dynamics, etc . . .)

Assessment
Organisation Form and structure of the advert. Have pupils kept to the brief (duration, completion deadline, etc)?
Creativity Interest and variety.
Use of resources Use of appropriate instruments, voices, sound effects.
Suitability of style Is the mood of the advert suitable for the target audience and the product to be advertised?
Pupils might like to discuss how successfully they think each advert would sell the product and why. For example, is the advert striking . . . is there a memorable 'catch phrase' or melody, etc?

The aim of this project is to create a sound tape to set the mood for a drama, or dance production. It could be played before, or during the performance. Alternatively, if no such production is likely, the project might provide a sound score for a short video sequence (about 2 mins). This could easily be recorded minus the sound and shown to the pupils at the start of the project. Suspense and horror movies provide rich material!

Cross-curricular links
Dance, Drama, and English departments if making music for a school production. Media Studies department for film sound tracks, and the Art department if you wish to explore visual images.

SETTING THE MOOD

When composers are asked to write some music that sets the mood to a play or a film, they are either shown some of the unedited film, or in the case of a stage production, a script.

The composer's job is to create some sound that will instantly set the mood for the audience. Usually this has to be done very quickly which is why a lot of film music is composed straight on to tape.

You will need to ask the following questions about the production or film and decide if the music needs to reflect any of these aspects.

What is the music for? (A play, a film, an exhibition such as a dungeon in a waxworks museum . . .)
What basic mood do you need to create?
Is the setting in the future, present, or past?
Where is the geographical location, somewhere in this country, somewhere abroad, on another planet, in someone's mind, in a dream . . . ?
Does the music have to last for a particular amount of time?
Are there any points where the music has to change? (For example, the film might suddenly cut to a picture that needs a loud chord, or perhaps a sudden scream to shock the audience! You will need to time the film so that you know exactly where in the music to put this.)

Once you have decided or been told what the music is for, you will need to select some sounds.

What types of sound will create the mood you need? Here is a list of different types of sound which might help:

LOUD	**QUIET**	**SUDDEN**	**GRADUAL**
LONG			**HIGH PITCHED**
SHORT			**LOW PITCHED**
WAVERING	**FALLING**	**RISING**	**CONSTANT**

Try choosing some suitable combinations that will help set the mood.

How about this one? It's a loud, low-pitched, long sound that gets higher . . .

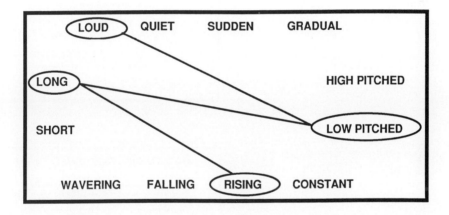

What instruments or voice sounds are you going to use?

Voice sounds can be very effective at setting a mood. Moaning, laughing, screaming, breath sounds are all stock effects for mood music. An echo or reverb box will make the sounds even more creepy!

You might find some useful sounds on the synthesiser. Some models have banks of 'effects' sounds with names such as 'Nightmare' and 'Ominous'.

Remember you can build up layers of sound using the four tracks, or keep one sound going while you play another over the top of it. Film composers always plan their music using a track sheet with frames of film, or minutes and seconds marked out. You may find it useful to do the same. Here is a plan for a short section in a horror film:

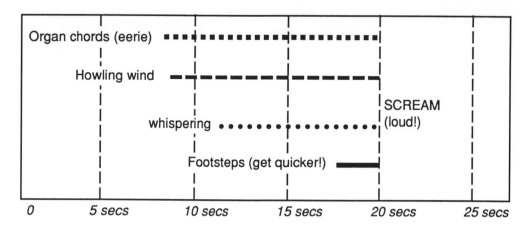

Organ chords (eerie)

Howling wind

whispering

SCREAM (loud!)

Footsteps (get quicker!)

| 0 | 5 secs | 10 secs | 15 secs | 20 secs | 25 secs |

The soundtrack starts with some eerie organ chords, so that's the sound to record first on track 1.

Recording Tracksheet

Track 1   eerie organ
Track 2
Track 3
Track 4

The second sound to record is the howling wind on track 2.

Recording Tracksheet

Track 1   eerie organ
Track 2   howling wind
Track 3
Track 4

This could be followed by the whispering recorded on track 3.

Recording Tracksheet

Track 1   eerie organ
Track 2   howling wind
Track 3   whispering | scream
Track 4

The footsteps could be recorded on track 4, and everything stops suddenly after 20 secs. After a pause of 1 second, there is a loud scream! This could be recorded on any of the tracks because everything else has stopped, but since it's another vocal sound we should probably record it on the same track as the whispering – that's track 3.

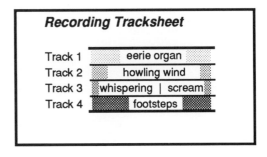

Recording Tracksheet

Track 1	eerie organ
Track 2	howling wind
Track 3	whispering | scream
Track 4	footsteps

Try planning your own piece of mood music and then begin to record it.

Follow-up work

Listen to some music used to accompany a radio play, TV play, or film. Try watching the TV or film pictures without the sound turned up first and ask what type of music the pupils would use before hearing how the composer interpreted the material. What types of sound have been used? What types of chord have been used? Has the use of dynamics, meter and tempo contributed to the building of a particular mood? Invite critical response. Pupils may wish to devise graphic notation to plan or document their work. (Many vocal sounds or sound effects would be impossible to notate in any other way!) A graphic score could easily be based on the pupil's tracksheet.

Assessment

Imaginative choice of available resources including voices.

Appropriate use of sounds to create the intended mood.

Inventiveness of the sounds: have available resources been used to their full potential, such as special vocal effects or effective use of the pitch-bend control on a synthesiser?

Control of mood and overall structure: e.g. building, releasing or sustaining tension. How well has the original brief been followed?

The basic principle behind Systems Music is to devise a 'system' or rule which is used to develop a simple musical idea. This project is suitable for pupils working in small groups, in pairs, or individually although the concept of Systems Music could be introduced within a whole class session. Pupils might use a range of tuned instruments, or perhaps their voices, with each pupil singing his own repeated pattern to a basic pulse.

Cross-curricular links
Systems Music within Western society is often based on mathematical processes. It is often recorded using computer music software. Within school there may be links to areas of the Maths curriculum: mathematical patterns, sequences, etc.

MAKING SYSTEMS MUSIC

You can make this short piece of Systems Music using a keyboard, a pitched instrument, or your voice. Composers have used hundreds of 'systems' or rules to make their music. Here is one simple example. The 'system' or rule behind this music is:

every new part adds one note to the previous phrase, and is played quicker.

First of all we need to choose four notes that sound good when played together. Try these or select your own group of notes.

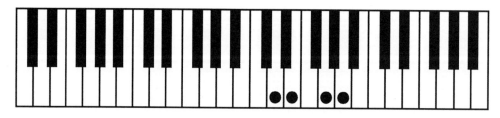

C D E F G A B C D E F G A B C D E F G A B C D E F G A B

Choose any one of the notes and play it repeatedly about once every second. (Don't play it too slowly though!) Keep the speed the same at all times; it's not as easy as it sounds. If you find this a problem try playing with a metronome or drum machine 'click track' set to about 70. Suppose you chose the note D, you would be playing this:

D   D   D   D

which is written like this in music notation:

When you are ready record your one note pulse on to track 1 of the tape. Play for about one minute.

Recording Tracksheet

Track 1	Pulse
Track 2	
Track 3	
Track 4	

Now let's use the system to make up the next part and record it on to track 2. Remember the system is to add one more note to the previous phrase. You've already used one of the four notes, so you have three left. Choose a new note and add it to the pulse. Practise playing the new 2-note phrase at double the speed of the pulse.

Suppose you now choose the note A, you would play this:

listen to Track 1	**Pulse**	D		D		D		D
play these notes:		D	A	D	A	D	A	D	A

This is the music notation for the new, repeating 2-note phrase:

When you can keep in time to the pulse on track 1, record this new part on to track 2. Wait until you have heard the pulse four times before starting:

	1	2	3	4				
listen to *Track 1*	D	D	D	D	D	D	D	D
record on *Track 2*	**Count 4 pulses then play:**			**D A D A D A D A**				

Recording Tracksheet

Track 1	Pulse
Track 2	2-note pattern
Track 3	
Track 4	

The next part will be made from three notes, the two you have just used plus one more, and you must play the phrase three times as fast, so all three notes must fit into the time of one pulse note. Suppose you now chose G as your 3rd note, you would play this:

	Pulse				
listen to *Track 1*		D	D	D	D
(switch off *Track 2)*					
play these **notes:**		**D A G D A G D A G D A G**			

This is the music notation for this repeating 3-note phrase:

Record this part on track 3 after you have heard the pulse eight times. You will find it easier to turn off track 2 for the moment and concentrate on playing your three notes to the pulsé.

> ### *Recording Tracksheet*
>
> Track 1   Pulse
> Track 2   2-note pattern
> Track 3   3-note pattern
> Track 4   _____

The last part will use all four notes and be played at four times the speed of the pulse on track 1. This is getting quite fast now, so you may need to practise a bit! This is what you might play:

	Pulse	D		D		D			D		
listen to Track 1											
(switch off Track 2)											
(switch off Track 3)											
play these notes:		D A G E	D A G E	D A G E	D A G E						

It's written in music notation like this:

Again you will find it easier to turn off tracks 2 and 3 and concentrate on playing to the pulse. Record the part on track 4 of the tape and start playing after you have counted twelve pulses.

Recording Tracksheet	
Track 1	Pulse
Track 2	2 note pattern
Track 3	3 note pattern
Track 4	4 note pattern

When you have finished, turn all the tracks back on and listen to the result. Check to see if it follows this plan . . . (fade out the tape before the end):

System Music Plan

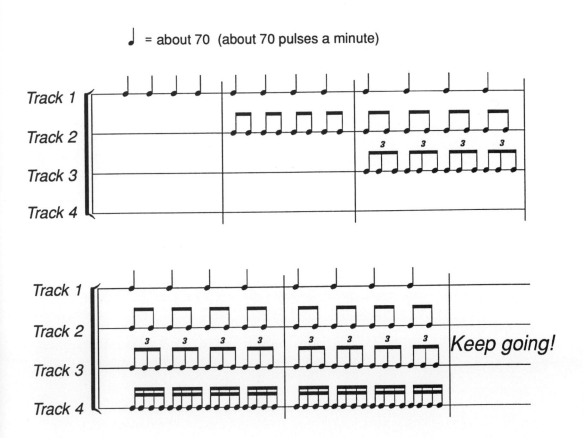

Congratulations! You have just produced a piece of Systems Music. You could make up your own piece of Systems Music now. You will probably need to make a plan of the piece in advance. These are some of the things you might decide before you begin.

Are you going to use one group of notes throughout or do you want to change them at certain points?

Are you going to play to a strict pulse or play freely?

What rhythms are you going to use? Here are some examples using the same four notes as before. You could use some of these or make up some new ones. Ask your teacher to play them to you and explain the new musical symbols: accents, ties and rests.

What instruments are you going to use? Do you want a drum part?

How are you going to begin – start separately, together, fade the tape in . . . ?

How loud are you going to play – the same throughout, or are there going to be changes?

How are you going to end – together, in reverse order to how you started, fade the tape . . . ?

Follow-up work

Listen to Systems Music by composers such as Steve Reich, John Adams or Terry Riley. Groups such as Lost Jockey use systems to make their songs. Can pupils hear the systems being used?

Assessment

Systems Music can be difficult to assess because you need to know the rules used and the objective. Pupils should be encouraged to make these clear as soon as possible. For example, if the pupil's intent is to produce a very mechanical piece without dynamic variation, then any assessment should take into account the fulfilment of this objective.

There will be opportunities to assess the process of making the piece from planning stage to final recording and the 'Composition Diary' sheet may be a useful way of keeping a record of the process. If appropriate, you might consider such aspects as:

Consistency of style.

Instrumentation: use of available instruments and voices.

Rhythmic variety.

Harmonic changes.

Overall structure of the composition: form, harmonic and rhythmic development, tempo changes, changes of instrumentation.

Here are four different ways to start making a Rap track. It's worth using the portastudio from the start so you can try out new ideas over your first recordings.

STARTING WITH THE BEAT

Rappers use several different ways of making the basic beat: these might include using a pre-programmed drum beat on an electronic keyboard, using a drum machine to programme a new beat, using real percussion instruments or using the voice. You can create a beat with the voice by blowing into a vocal microphone to produce the bass drum sound and using your voice to produce vocal versions of other drumlike sounds. This is called Human Beatbox and you might like to experiment with this technique. Some rappers use a combination of electronic, acoustic and vocal sounds.

What is a Rap Beat?
Here's a very simple rap beat. You'll see that the pattern (musicians call this a bar) is split into four main beats. Each beat is further divided into four. If you have a programmable drum machine, try making a beat by programming in the following instruments on the points of the bar shown.

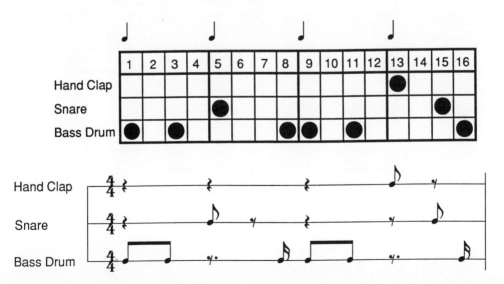

Try a speed of crotchet equals 96 to start with. If that feels too slow, speed up the drum machine.

Of course this drum beat is just a starting idea and you will probably want to make up your own personal beats. It's a good idea to make up several alternative beats or 'fills' because playing exactly the same pattern over and over again will get a little monotonous. Try programming these and alternate them with your first beat:

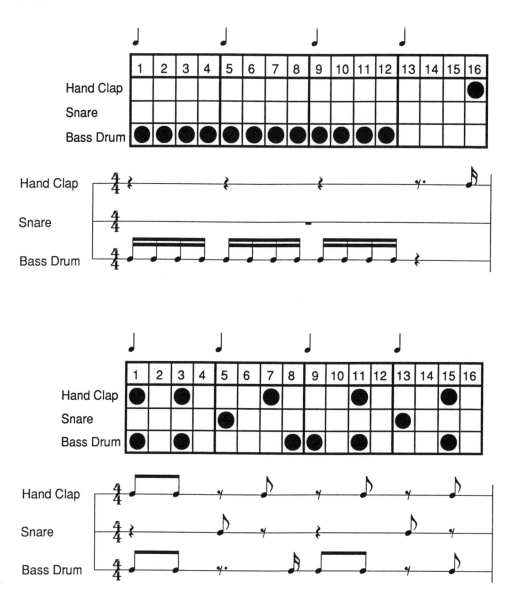

Try combinations of these to build up a complete song. You could record the patterns on to track 1 of the portastudio and then try out some words or effects with the beat.

There are only two rules about the words: they will need to be very rhythmic and they will need to rhyme at the end of phrases.

Here is an example of the opening line to a rap:

1	2	3	4	5	6	7	8	9	10	11	12	13	14	15	16
														I	was

1	2	3	4	5	6	7	8	9	10	11	12	13	14	15	16
walk	-ing	down	the	street		just	the	oth-	er			day,		saw	

1	2	3	4	5	6	7	8	9	10	11	12	13	14	15	16
M.		C.		Dee		was		head-	ing	my		way			

Some Rappers and MCs improvise with their lyrics but most usually work out a large part of the performance before going in front of the audience.

If more than one person is rapping, then you will need to work out the order in which you perform and the places where you all rap the same words together.

Very slick rappers sometimes alternate words, or use a question and answer routine:

1	2	3	4	5	6	7	8	9	10	11	12	13	14	15	16
														● Hey	

Rapper 1

1	2	3	4	5	6	7	8	9	10	11	12	13	14	15	16
●		●		●		○	○	○	○	○		○			

Rapper 1 you! (col 1)

Rapper 2 what (col 3) — me? (col 5)

Rapper 3 Now (col 7) — just (col 8) — have (col 9) — a (col 10) — nice (col 11) — day! (col 13)

Starting with some Sound Effects

The most common effect is Scratching. This is the sound made when a record is moved quickly backwards and forwards by about an inch with the stylus still in the record groove. To do this you need to use a 'slip mat' on the turntable. This is a piece of felt placed on the turntable underneath the record. When it is held it stops the record from spinning while still allowing the turntable to revolve underneath.

If you don't have a record deck it's possible to produce scratching sounds on some synthesisers. Look to see if you have a synthesiser with a scratch patch!

Rappers use other effects such as explosions, whooshes, ghostly whistles, etc. If you have an Effects Unit you may be able to make electronic voice sounds such as robots or martians.

You will either need to decide where in the lyrics these effects occur, or base your lyrics around the sound effects.

If you record your effects on to one track of the portastudio, and your lyrics on to another, you will have total control and be able to change or re-record either of them if they don't quite work together the first time.

Starting with some Music Ideas

Rappers often take small parts of other records and use them throughout the rap. If you have a Sampler you could sample a small section of a record and play it back at different speeds and pitches.

Alternatively you could record some short sections of another record on to one of the tape tracks. You could even change the speed and pitch by recording with the pitch control on. (If you record with the speed control set faster, the final recording will be slower and lower, if you record with the speed control slower, then the result will sound faster and higher.)

Instead of using bits of other records you may want to make up your own music. Try making a bass line that you can play throughout the rap. You could do this with a bass guitar, the bass end of an electronic keyboard, or a synthesiser. Stick to a few notes and give them the same type of rhythm as the drum beat. If you like, try this example using these notes for your bass line:

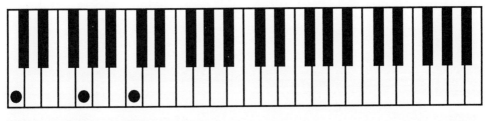

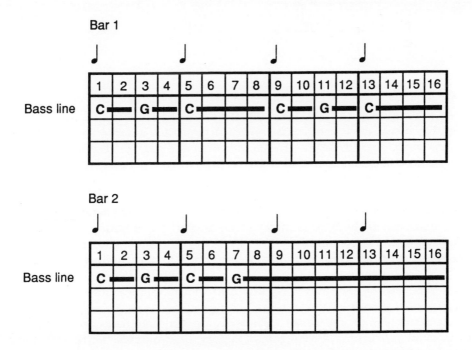

Bass

Follow-up work

Pupils might like to develop variations on the bass line rather than repeat the same pattern over and over again. Suggest the use of all the notes in the scale (as 'passing notes'). Transposition could also be introduced.

The bass line could make use of some of the rhythmic patterns used in the drum and vocal parts.

Bass

Pupils may wish to find some chords to play with the bass line, and these could be recorded on a spare track if one is available. When playing back the finished recording, pupils may wish to use the faders or track replay switches to cut the backing tracks in and out at various points in the rap. For example, pupils may wish to cut the drums and bass for a section where there is a vocal 'punchline'. See Chapter 3 on Mixing.

Assessment

Appropriate use of rhythms to match the words.

Variety of vocal rhythms.

Inventiveness of the vocal track: e.g. use of questions and answers, chorus and solo sections, different types of voices.

Drum part: use of appropriate rhythm patterns to complement the voice parts, variety of rhythm patterns, consistency of style.

Appropriate selection and use of 'borrowed' musical material.

Use of available resources: selection of suitable instruments.

Appropriate use of chords and/or bass line.

CHAPTER 11

MUSIC FROM AFRICA

This project will introduce the idea of cross rhythms such as groups of two against groups of three, or alternating sections of groups of two and three. Using the portastudio, pupils will be able to make complex rhythmic structures part by part.

This project is about using one rhythmic idea found in some African music. Although pupils will not be playing authentic African music, the project may encourage them to seek out and listen to the real thing.

Cross-curricular links
Art and Home Economics departments may be making use of visual patterns that rely on overlaying simple designs to produce complex results. This project may link with work in the Geography department.

INFLUENCE OF AFRICAN RHYTHMS

African music has influenced a lot of musicians all over the world. The exciting drum and percussion patterns used by African musicians seem very complicated at first, but they are made by the musicians playing several simple patterns at the same time. This produces 'cross-rhythms' (rhythms that literally 'cross over' each other) as the individual patterns mix together.

THE BEAT TRACK

Let's make some music using cross-rhythms. First you need a steady pulse to accompany the rhythms. You could either use a drum machine or a metronome. Set the speed to about 70 beats per minute (that's $\quad$ = 70) and record the pulse on to track 1 of the portastudio.

Recording Tracksheet

Track 1   Pulse

Track 2   _____

Track 3   _____

Track 4   _____

Next you need to decide what instruments to use for the rest of the beat track. You could use the toms of a drum kit, or congas. If you decide to use a drum machine, play the sounds 'live'. It is quite difficult to programme cross-rhythms on most drum machines.

Practise playing one of these rhythms. They are all based on two beats to the pulse and are written in music notation so you may need to ask someone to play them to you!

Now try playing one of the following in time with the pulse:

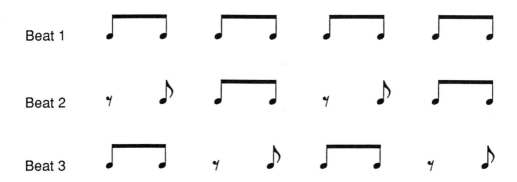

When you can play the rhythm and repeat it, listen to the pulse on track 1 and try playing in time with it. When you are ready, record it on to track 2 of the portastudio.

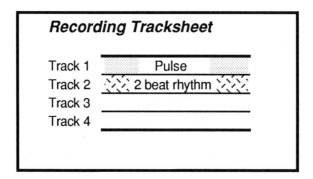

When you are happy with your recording, turn off track 2 so that all you can hear is the pulse on track 1 again. Now choose one of the following rhythms which are all based on three beats to every pulse.

Pulse

Try playing one of the following in time with the pulse:

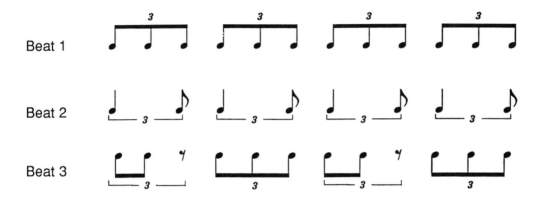

Beat 1

Beat 2

Beat 3

Practise playing it along with the pulse. You may find you need to clear the previous rhythm out of your head before you can do this! When you are ready, record the rhythm on to track 3.

Recording Tracksheet

Track 1	Pulse
Track 2	2 beat rhythm
Track 3	3 beat rhythm
Track 4	

If you play back tracks 2 and 3 together you should be able to hear a typical cross-rhythm beat.

MAKING MORE SPACE ON THE TAPE

So far, three of the four tape tracks have been used. If you want to record more than one more track, you will need to make more space on the tape by merging some of the tracks. This is called 'bouncing' tracks. Let's 'bounce' or merge tracks 2 and 3 on to track 4. This will free tracks 2 and 3 for recording more music.

This is how to merge or 'bounce' the tracks:

First tell mixer channels 2 and 3 to replay tracks 2 and 3 of the tape.
Pan channels 2 and 3 fully to the right.
Make sure mixer channel 1 fader is down so there is no chance of bouncing the pulse as well. The controls will look something like this:

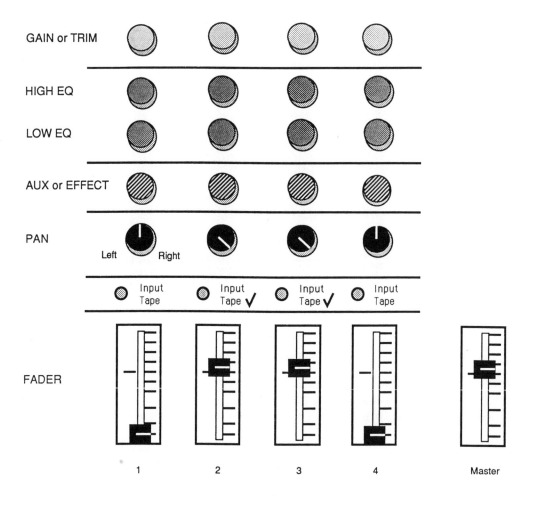

You will need to set the equalisation controls on channels 2 and 3 to get the best sound. Adjust the level of each track with the faders.

Now tell track 4 to record everything panned to the right – see Chapters 2 and 3. (Make sure all the other tracks are set to safe!)

You are ready to record.

Play back track 4 to check the result. Make sure that tracks 2 and 3 are turned off because the original recordings are still on the tape. If you don't like the mix on track 4, try again! When you are happy with the recording on track 4, you can then record new parts on to tracks 2 and 3.

THE CHORDS

You could use a keyboard, synthesiser, organ, piano, guitar, or xylophones to record some basic chords on to track 2.

Try these chords on the instrument.

C major chord

CDEFGABCDEFGABCDEFGABCDEFGAB

F major chord

CDEFGABCDEFGABCDEFGABCDEFGAB

G major chord

CDEFGABCDEFGABCDEFGABCDEFGAB

Now listen to the pulse on track 1, and try playing the chords to the pulse and in the following order:

listen to Track 1	Pulse	♩	♩	♩	♩
play these:	Chords	C	C	F ▬▬▬▬▬	

	Pulse	♩	♩	♩	♩
	Chords	C	C	G ▬▬▬▬▬	

When you are ready, record the chords on to track 2.

Recording Tracksheet

Track 1	Pulse
Track 2	chords
Track 3	
Track 4	2 and 3 beat rhythms

In Africa the musicians wouldn't stop there. They might play the chords on several instruments to make more cross-rhythms. Here's a simple way to add to the chord part.

Tap out the three beats to the pulse rhythm on the tape, don't bother tapping the pulse. Now make the first tap in every three louder than the others: try tapping the loud beat (shown as a dark blob) with your left hand and the others (shown as grey blobs) with your right hand.

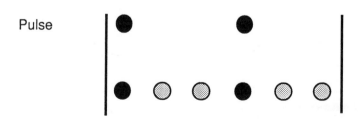

Pulse

Now try keeping exactly the same speed for each tap, but make the first tap of every two louder. (Again play the loud taps with your left hand and the others with your right hand.)

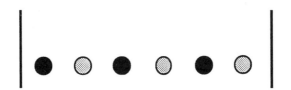

Now try tapping them after each other:

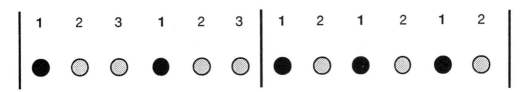

You can play the chords in this way. You will probably find it easier to use two hands, the left hand to play the loud beat and the right hand to play the others. Look at the keyboard chords.

Play the lowest note of the chord with the left hand and one or both of the others with your right hand. This is how it is written in music notation, so ask someone to show you on the keyboard if you can't work it out!

right hand

left hand

When you are ready record these rhythm chords on to track 3.

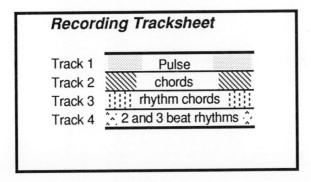

Follow-up work
● Pupils might wish to continue with the composition by adding an instrumental or vocal melody line. This could easily be recorded on track 1 (the pulse would of course be erased, but by this stage the rhythm should be established and there should be no further need for a guide track).
● Pupils may wish to develop their rhythmic skills by exploring more complex cross-rhythms than those given in this project. Possible areas of exploration might include further subdivisions of the basic pulse, for example 3-groups (triplets) against 5-groups (quintuplets). Alternatively they may work with different sub-divisions of a bar. For example a bar of 8 eighth notes (quavers) could be divided alternately into groups of 5 + 3, 4 + 2 + 2, or 3 + 3 + 2. Rhythms of increasing complexity might make use of sixteenth notes (semiquavers), dotted notes and tied notes.

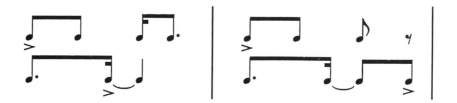

● Patterns could also be played offset against themselves by an eighth note as shown:

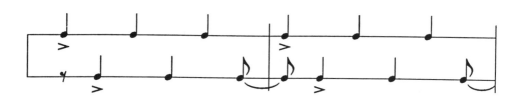

Assessment
Accuracy and imaginative use of rhythm. Development of rhythmic ideas and cross-rhythms.
Selection and inventive use of chords.
Development of 'rhythm chords' and of a melody line.

WHY KEEP RECORDS?

Keeping a written record of what is recorded on each of the four tracks will help pupils remember where each part of the music is, and will be especially useful when pupils have to leave a project unfinished between lessons.

Some records can be used by other pupils. For example, you might decide to build up a library of record sheets giving details of where to place microphones when recording acoustic instruments or singers. Every time a recording works particularly well, a copy of the record sheet could be added to the library. When at some future time other pupils need to record the same acoustic instrument, they will be able to refer to the library. This should help everyone make better recordings and save a lot of time.

WHAT SORT OF RECORDS ARE USEFUL?

1 *A Tracksheet* is used to write down what is recorded on each track of tape. Pupils should be encouraged to keep an up-to-date record of all their recording work on one of these. They could include details of the portastudio control settings, such as any equalisation used, together with which instrument was used. The names and numbers of any electronic keyboard and synthesiser sounds should be written down in case pupils need to rework part of the composition. Tracksheets will provide useful documentation to help pupils reflect on a piece of work and may be useful to include in a GCSE submission or a Record of Achievement folder.
2 *A Set Up Sheet* is a written record of how microphones were set up. They consist of a diagram showing where in the room the musicians were playing, which microphones were used and where they were placed.
3 *The Cassette Inlay Card* Keeping a record with each cassette tape giving details of recordings on the tape and the date on which they were started will help you to avoid taping over something you want to keep. For absolute safety, number or mark the cassette, the cassette case, and the card inside the case. Then list all the recordings with names of pupils and recording dates. This may sound like a chore to begin with, but when you only have one afternoon left before a GCSE entry deadline you'll be glad you took the trouble. You may even persuade the pupils to do a lot of it for you!
4 *Pupils' Personal List of Recordings* One of these can be kept in each pupil's work folder and all recordings listed with dates, titles, and which tape the recording is on. This type of sheet can encourage pupils to think about giving each composition a meaningful title. Many pupils tend to name their compositions 'Keyboard Piece 1', 'Keyboard Piece 2' . . . or 'Tracy 1', 'Tracy 2', etc. These names can be

very unhelpful descriptions when, at the end of the course, a portfolio of work has to be assembled.

5 *Pupils' Individual Evaluation Sheet*   You may already use this type of record to help pupils evaluate their previous work and negotiate future projects. The examples here are a pupil/teacher assessment record and a composition diary to enable pupils and/or teachers to record brief notes at each stage of a composition's development.

You are welcome to copy and use the tracksheet, set up sheet, cassette inlay card and other record sheets included in this chapter. Alternatively you or the pupils may decide to design your own, perhaps with the help of other departments within the school. For example, pupils might design a tracksheet as part of a design project, possibly using a computer graphics programme. If you do make your own, here are some of the things you might also want to include:

On a tracksheet:
Name of Composer(s) and Performer(s).
Date the recording was started.
The name or number of the cassette tape.
Where on the tape the recording begins (tape counter number).
The Instruments and Voices recorded on each track.
The types of Microphone used.
The names or numbers of sounds used on a synthesiser or electronic keyboard.
Which model of keyboard (if you have several different types).
The Tape Speed if your machine has more than one.
Noise Reduction on or off.

On a set up sheet:
A rough sketch of the layout if mics were used.
Details of the instruments recorded.
Where the mics were positioned and the type of mics used.
Any Effects that were used.
Comments on the quality of the sound recorded from each instrument.

RECORDING TRACKSHEET

TAPE NUMBER	

TITLE	
COMPOSED BY	
DATE	

1	
2	
3	
4	

TAPE COUNTER	

NOISE REDUCTION	IN / OUT
TAPE SPEED	HIGH / LOW

This page may be copied for your own use

RECORDING SET UP SHEET

DATE	TITLE

TAPE NUMBER

PERFORMERS:

DIAGRAM and DETAILS:

NOTES:

This page may be copied for your own use

CASSETTE INLAY CARD

STEREO	4 TRACK	Dolby	DBX

Counter	Title	Composer	Date

Fold here

Fold here

Fold here

This page may be copied for your own use

RECORDING PORTFOLIO

Name: _____

Title of Recording	Date started	Date Finished	Tape Number or Name

This page may be copied for your own use

PUPIL ASSESSMENT RECORD

Name: Tutor: Date:

Achievements

Pupil's own Comments

Areas for Development

Negotiated Aims

Teacher's Comment on:

Attendance
Motivation
Participation
Homework

This page may be copied for your own use

Name

COMPOSITION DIARY: PAGE 1

		Provisional title:
Date:	**Discussion notes:**	

Date:	
	Initial Ideas: (instrumentation, theme, form, duration, style...)
	Achievements to date: Next stage:
	Achievements to date: Next stage:
	Achievements to date: Next stage:

This page may be copied for your own use

Name

COMPOSITION DIARY: PAGE 2

Date:	Discussion notes:
	Achievements to date: Next stage:
	Achievements to date: Next stage:
	Achievements to date: Next stage:
	Final discussion notes: Documentation: plans, score.... Recording:

This page may be copied for your own use

PART THREE
REFERENCE

Microphones come in all shapes and sizes. Some are intended for general use while others are made for a specific application. For example, there are microphones made for singers to use on stage. These are sensitive to sounds at very close range without picking up too much background sound. If you used one of these microphones to record a group of quiet xylophones the results would not be very good.

Microphone manufacturers produce brochures that clearly say what each model of microphone is best at recording and there are suitable microphones available at reasonable prices for most school situations.

There are some general categories of microphone which offer clues on which one to use. Let's look first at the area in which you might expect a microphone to pick up sound.

There are two main categories – 'omnidirectional' mics that pick up sound coming from all directions, and 'directional' mics which will record sound in specific areas only.

OMNIDIRECTIONAL

These record everything around them, in front as well as behind. This type of microphone would be very unhelpful in many school situations where there is a certain amount of background noise, from other groups or rooms for example. If there's not too much noise outside they are good at recording a whole class performance. The shaded areas in these diagrams show where the mic will pick up sound:

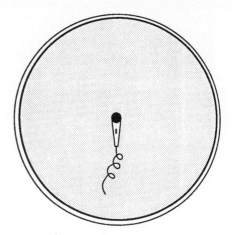

DIRECTIONAL

The most common types are:

Cardioid
These directional microphones record mainly what's in front of them so are good for recording small groups or individual instruments in the classroom.

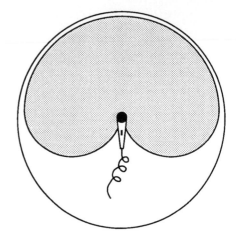

Hypercardioid
Similar to Cardioid microphones, they record sounds in front of them and are good at recording small groups in the classroom.

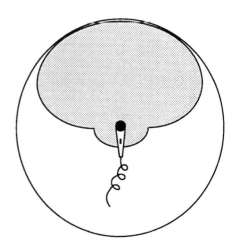

Figure of Eight
These record immediately in front and behind, but not from either side and are ideal for interviews.

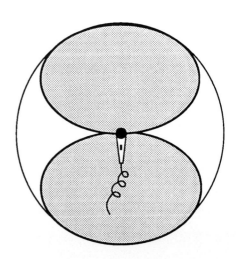

Microphones are also categorised by the way they transform sound into electrical signals. Let's look at the most common types:

DYNAMIC microphones respond well to loud levels of sound and are useful for close miking of drum kits – especially bass drums. The cheaper ones tend to record well in the mid-frequency range but not so well at the high (treble) and low (bass) extremes.

However the fact that dynamic microphones record some types of sound better than others can be put to good use. Some slightly more expensive ones are particularly good in the treble range (between 3 and 8kHz for the technically minded) which makes them ideal for recording clear vocals.

ELECTRET CONDENSER microphones are cheap versions of the Condensers used in professional studios. They need internal batteries and produce good quality sound especially at the treble end.

In school they are excellent for recording ensembles of quiet classroom instruments. They would also be ideal for recording orchestras and choirs.

Don't use them for close-up recording because they tend to distort at loud sound levels and don't like rough treatment.

CONDENSER microphones are best suited to studio use. They give an excellent response over the entire audio range. Condenser microphones are normally powered by a small voltage sent down the mic cable from the mixer. As portastudios are unable to send condensers a power supply, this together with their expensive price tag makes them unsuitable for classroom use.

PZM (Pressure Zone Microphones) have only been around for a few years and are very different from traditional microphones in look and in the way you use them.

A PZM is a small rectangular sheet of metal with a small electret microphone fixed on it. They need to be mounted on a large surface such as a wall or board. (Blu-tack is fine for mounting the PZM.) The smaller the surface on which the PZM is mounted, the less bass sound the mic will pick up.

Tandy produce a very good but cheap PZM for about £30. One word of warning, PZMS are remarkably good at picking up everything, which doesn't always make them ideal for noisy or reverberant surroundings like classrooms!

CONTACT microphones are useful for getting a strong signal from acoustic instruments. Often the microphone is fitted permanently to the instrument although 'stick on' contact mics are now available. The sound from a contact mic is always different from that achieved by conventional microphones.

RADIO microphones are useful for live stage work, or for 'outside broadcast' situations. These microphones use a small radio transmitter instead of a cable and are more flexible if performers need to move around a lot. Unfortunately they sometimes 'drift' (like a radio receiver not being tuned properly) and they have a nasty habit of picking up local radio-controlled taxi-cabs at inopportune moments!

Radio mics are not particularly cheap, but they can be hired.

SOME IDEAS ON WHERE TO POINT MICROPHONES

When using directional microphones, the basic principle is simple: find where the sound comes out of the instrument and aim the microphone in that direction!

The distance between the mic and the sound source will have an effect on the quality of the recorded sound as well as the loudness. In general the closer the mic, the more bass will be recorded. The further away, the more 'atmosphere' and the less instrument.

Mic stands are worth their weight in gold! The ones with stand and boom arm are much more flexible than the 'floor stand only' variety.

Finally, keep a record of which mics you set up and where you positioned them.

Here are some examples of how to set about recording specific instruments. Use them as starting points and feel free to experiment. If the instrument you want to record is not listed, try to find one that is similar.

Acoustic Guitar   Aim the mic directly at the sound hole from about 6 to 12 inches away.

Electric Guitar   No mic required! Use a jack lead to plug the guitar straight into the multitrack. If the volume isn't loud enough, use the MIC setting instead of the LINE setting.

Electric Guitar through a **Combo**   Place the mic so that it's almost touching the speaker grill and a little to one side of the speaker cone (the round thing behind the grill).

Electronic Keyboard   For the best results, don't bother with a mic but use a jack lead to plug it straight into the multitrack. Use the LINE input setting. If for some reason you need to record via a Combo, set up as for the Guitar and Combo above.

Brass, also **Nadhaswaram** and **Saxophone**   Point the mic into the bell of the instrument at a distance of about 9 inches. For a fuller sound, or less breath noise, place the mic slightly further away.

Woodwind including **Algoza** and **Indian Flute**   Place the mic above the player's head and pointing down towards the finger holes.

Violin   Place the mic above the instrument pointing down at the sound holes at a distance of 1 to 2 feet. A closer distance will accentuate the sound of the bow on string.

Sitar, Cello and **Double-bass, Iktara** and **Tamboura**   Place the mic to point at the bridge for a bright sound, or the sound holes for a fuller sound.

Piano (upright)   Try setting the mic behind the piano. You may need two mics, one for the top strings, the other around the middle. Alternatively open the lid and point the mic at the top end.

Piano (grand)   With the lid open, set up the microphone at the back right-hand side (as the player sees it) and pointing at the strings. (You may get a better sound with two mics, pointing at the high and middle strings.)

If you have a PZM, try sticking it on the open piano lid, underneath, of course, not on top!

Drum Kit   There are no rules! If you have only one or two mics then place them above the player's head, one pointing at the left-hand part of the kit, the other at the right.

If you have one PZM, try sticking it on a wall about 1 meter in front of the drum kit.

If you have more mics at your disposal then try the following . . .

A mic inside the Bass drum (you may need to remove the front drum head if it hasn't got a hole cut in it) resting on a cushion or someone's jacket, and aimed slightly off centre at the drum head. If you pick up any squeaks from the drum pedal, oil it!

Point a mic at the top head of the Snare drum near to the rim.

Careful placing will enable you to record the Hi-hat on the same mic, but you need to take care that it isn't too prominent. If you intend using any effects with the Snare, mic up the Hi-hat separately. If you really do have 'loads of mics' then aim another at the lower head of the Snare drum to give the sound more punch.

Aim one or two mics at the Toms from above. You may need to place them below the Cymbals if these sound too prominent on the tape. If you *still* have mics and input channels to spare you're probably not using a 4-track cassette at all! Aim a mic at the floor Tom from about 9 inches above.

A 'tighter' sound will be achieved when recording the kit with individual mics on each drum if Noise Gates (see Chapter 14) are used on the Bass and Snare drums.

Small Percussion, Tabla Aim the mic at any sound holes or jingles if there are any. Otherwise place the mic overhead pointing down at the instrument. Try a distance of 12 inches and experiment if it doesn't sound right.

Solo Vocalist Encourage the vocalist to leave the mic on the stand. Holding a mic can introduce a lot of unwelcome noise on to the tape, but if for any reason the vocalist really does need to hold it, try looping the cable and holding the loop against the mic. At least this will cut down on cable noise. If possible, use a mic with a windshield to cut down on breath noise.

The closer the mic to the vocalist's mouth, the more bass will be recorded – that's to say the voice will sound deeper. Unfortunately the closer the mic, the more likely it is to 'pop' on 'p's, 'b's, and 'd's. A solution to this is to sing, speak or rap *across* the mic, not *into* it. Try setting the mic on a stand in front of the vocalist and pointing straight down at the floor with the windshield of the mic an inch above the vocalist's mouth. A bonus is that you can sellotape the words to the mic stand!

Several Singers If you have enough mics, group two or three singers around each mic and as close as possible. Alternatively point one mic at the entire group at a distance of 3 to 4 feet.

Choir Use two identical microphones (electrets if possible) and set them up in front of the choir at a distance of about 6 to 8 feet and at a height of 6 feet with one pointing towards the right-hand side of the choir, the other to the left.

Steel Pans For one, or a small group, set the mic overhead at a height of 2 feet for one pan, further away for several.

To record a Steel Band try setting up two identical mics at the front, one pointing towards the left, the other to the right. These should pick up the Ping Pong Pans. You may then need to put a mic above the Bass Pans and another above the Cello Pans. If a Drum Kit is being used you may find it doesn't need any mics on it at all because the other mics pick up enough of the kit sound.

RECORDING LIVE EVENTS

There is only one predictable thing about recording a live event: things will go wrong! Ask recording engineers for advice and they will probably tell you not to bother, so try not to rely totally on a live performance to record a good tape for an examination portfolio. There are, of course, situations where you have to record a live event, so here are some simple precautions you can take to stack the odds in your favour:

Record the last rehearsal and keep the tape.

Set your recording levels at previous rehearsals, but expect the performers to play or sing louder at the concert than at the rehearsal.

Check that the length of the performance will fit on to the tape. If not, prearrange a pause in the performance to take one tape out quickly and put a fresh tape in, (with the leader wound on.)

Use as few microphones as possible, but include a stereo pair (two identical mics at the front pointing to left and right). These will tend to record 'what the audience hears' and will probably give the best results.

Tape all exposed mic cables to the floor with strong gaffer tape.

Have a spare mic lead handy.

If there is an audience present then add these to the list:

Don't set up any equipment where it will be in the way of the audience.

In particular, don't set up mic stands within range of the audience's feet.

Tape all mic cables with extra strong gaffer tape and try to keep them out of the audience's way.

Buying Microphones – What to Look for

1 How robust does it look?
2 What use does the manufacturer suggest?
3 Is it low impedance? (High impedance mics are not suitable for most recording equipment.)
4 Is it directional?
5 Is it suitable for portastudio recording?
6 Is it a mono or stereo mic?
7 Is the cable included?
8 Does it require a battery?

Shure, AKG, Beyer, Sennheiser and Audio Technica are all reliable manufacturers whose products have been used in classrooms for years.

The problem with most 'school' recordings is that they have that 'classroom sound'. Not surprising since that's exactly where most of them have been recorded! One way of getting the best out of your portastudio is to use EFFECTS UNITS (sometimes called SIGNAL PROCESSORS, and not to be confused with 'sound effects'). Effects units are widely used in the recording of popular and classical music.

Some effects units can transform a sound into something completely different. Used more discreetly they are able to give a recording more sparkle and gloss. A few effects units are able to improve the quality of a recording by automatically controlling the level of sound and by getting rid of unwanted background noise, and these are particularly useful in the classroom.

Better Quality in the Classroom

These effects won't improve the quality of the composition, but the recording will sound a lot better!

NOISE GATE A very useful device when there's a lot of background noise, the Noise Gate can cut off a signal when it drops below a certain level of loudness. Here's how you could use it:

Put a noise gate on a microphone recording a singer and the gate will turn the mic off whenever the singer isn't singing.

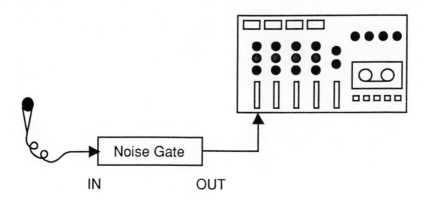

First set the 'threshold level'. The noise gate will only let through sounds that are louder than the threshold level. In the following diagram the threshold level of the noise gate has been set to stop the recording of unwanted noise in the pauses such as the singer's coughing or rustling the lyric sheets, and the second-year class next door. When the vocalist starts singing, the voice is louder than the threshold level and all the sound is able to pass through the gate on to the tape. The singer is recorded, and hopefully the second-year class will be masked by the voice.

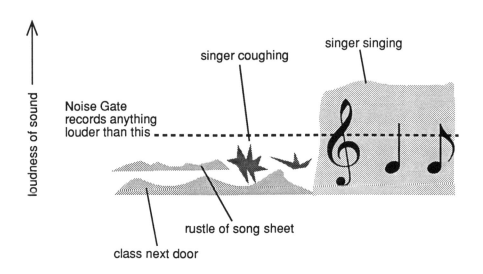

Similarly, if you are recording an electronic instrument that hisses or crackles a lot when not being played, a gate will just record the playing, and switch the signal off during the pauses.

The gate can also be used to tighten up the sound of instruments such as drums and bass guitar. It will chop off the end of the sound as it dies away.

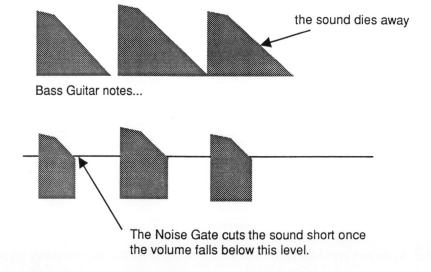

A gate is particularly useful when recording a drum kit with several mics. The bass drum mic, for example, will tend to pick up some of the rest of the kit when it's not recording the bass drum. This will contribute to a muddy sound.

Putting a gate on both bass drum and snare drum microphones will stop these mics picking up other parts of the kit, and produce a much clearer recording.

If your portastudio has an INSERT facility, then an alternative way to connect the noise gate would be like this:

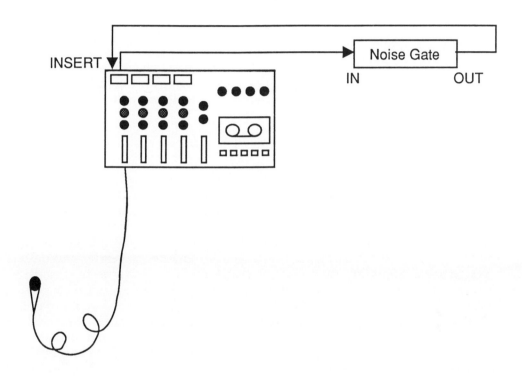

The Insert facility diverts all the sound coming into an input channel, sends it to an effects unit, and then returns it to the same input channel. You may need a special lead to do this.

COMPRESSOR A compressor 'squeezes' or 'irons out' the differences in dynamic level of a signal. Why should you want to do this? Here are two possible reasons:

RECORDING A SINGER Singers are notorious for moving around while recording. Unfortunately, moving just a few inches from the microphone can change the recording level from being very healthy to being almost inaudible. Using a compressor on the microphone will produce a steady recording level and save having to tie the singer to a chair.

RECORDING AN ORCHESTRA Tape recorders are still unable to record the full range of dynamics audible to the ear. If you are recording music which makes use of a wide range of dynamics (an orchestra for example) gentle use of a compressor will squeeze the range of dynamics so that the tape will pick up the very quiet parts while not distorting the very loud parts.

Compression is used widely in commercial music to maintain a high level of sound, which has the effect of giving the recording more 'punch'.

You can connect a compressor between the microphone or electronic instrument and the portastudio as in the Noise Gate example (p.91), or via the INSERT facility if your portastudio has one.

ADDING A TOUCH OF GLOSS

These effects will add gloss and sparkle to your recordings.

REVERB short for Reverberation   This is probably the most used effect commercially as it gives the impression of space. That's to say it makes something recorded in a dead room sound as if it happened in a hall, a large cathedral, a bathroom, or underneath some arches. Used with discretion it will transform music recorded with close mics in a classroom from a dull lifeless sound into one full of richness and life. It will give singers more confidence if they hear themselves with reverb and may improve the performance you are able to record on to tape.
ECHO   Usually called DIGITAL DELAY nowadays, this is probably the most overused effect; but it's good fun to experiment with, so why not!

Echo makes the sound repeat. You can usually set the speed of the repeats and the number of times the sound is repeated. Some echo boxes will 'freeze' a sound and repeat it for ever, or allow you to play the frozen sound at different pitches by connecting the unit to a keyboard.
CHORUS   This is used to 'fatten' the sound and is found extensively on synthesisers where manufacturers use it to disguise their otherwise thin-sounding products. Guitarists use it to disguise their cheap instruments and sometimes their playing too!

A Chorus unit takes the sound and doubles it up with a very slightly delayed version at a slightly differing pitch. It is very useful with guitars and vocals.
FLANGER   A flanger works in the same way as a chorus, but instead of processing the sound just once, it sends the sound back to the input stage to be processed again. The final effect will depend on the number of times the sound is fed back and can range from the huge sweeping and whooshing sounds loved by some guitarists to super chorus effects.
PHASER   This effect used to be made by playing two identical tapes or records and changing the speed of one by a microscopic amount. This produces a magic sweeping effect on the sound which is difficult to describe. Nowadays Phasing is done electronically.
EXCITER   Sometimes called an ENHANCER, an Exciter adds harmonics to a sound. This effect is used a lot in commercial studios to add some sparkle to a dull recording or to make one instrument 'stand out' from the rest.
PITCH SHIFTER   Play a sound through a Pitch Shifter and it will be 'transposed', although in a slightly 'electronic' form.

Pitch shifters usually transpose up or down by any amount up to an octave. Pitch shifters are good at harmonically thickening material when the transposed version is added to the sound at its original pitch. Without too much of the original sound they do great robots and space monsters!

How to use Effects

The question to ask is: do I want all the sound to go through the effects unit so that none of the original sound remains, or do I want to keep the original sound but add some of the effects to it?

When noise-gating or equalising a bass guitar you will need to send the entire signal through the effects unit without retaining any of the original sound because otherwise the original sound will mask the processed version. (The way to connect the effect to the portastudio is described in the Noise Gate section pp. 91–93.)

When adding reverb to a voice, usually you will want to add just a little to the original sound. Try sending all the sound through a reverb unit and the singer's voice will appear to be coming from the depths of a giant cave!

When mixing, the most convenient way of adding effects such as reverb to previously recorded tracks is to use the AUXILIARY SEND(s). You will then be able to add reverb to several tracks at the same time.

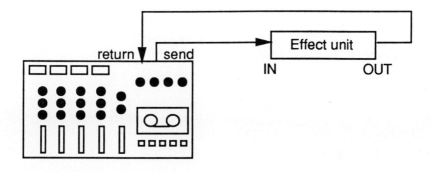

Use the AUX SEND and RETURN sockets to connect the effects unit. Find the AUX SEND socket on your portastudio and connect it to the input socket on the effects unit. Connect the output socket on the effects unit to the return socket on the portastudio.

The amount of sound you send to the effects unit will be controlled by the knobs marked EFFECT/AUX SEND. If your portastudio has an AUX SEND control on each mixer channel then you will be able to set different amounts of reverb on each track.

Buying Effects Units

There are two main types of effects unit available, 'multi effects' units and 'single effects' units.

Multi effects units are able to produce a range of effects, but you can usually use them on only one thing at a time. For example you could use a multi effect unit to put reverb and chorus on track 1, but you would need another unit to put echo on to another track at the same time.

Single effects units are able to produce one effect only, so you will need to buy a separate reverb, a separate echo, etc. The advantage of single effects units is that you can use them to put several effects on to more than one track at the same time. You could also chain them together, that's to say put a sound through several units to make very complex effects.

Things to ask when buying Effects Units
1   How many effects can it do?
2   How many effects will it do at once?
3   Will it work with a portastudio? (Some effects units are intended for guitars only.)
4   Is there a microphone input?
5   Can you edit (personalise) the effects?
6   If you can edit the effects, can you then store them in the unit?
7   How is it powered? (Mains, power supply unit, batteries?)
8   Is it MIDI (important if you wish to control it with a MIDI instrument, or computer)?
9   Is it mono or stereo?

CHAPTER 15

IN THE CLASSROOM – MAKING CONNECTIONS

How to Hear the Portastudio

Before you use the portastudio in class, make sure you can hear what you are recording.

There are two ways to hear what you are doing. The first is to use loudspeakers, the second is to use headphones.

1 Connecting the portastudio to Speakers
If you use the loudspeaker method you will need to connect your portastudio to an amplifier and speakers. A stereo hi-fi system would be best.

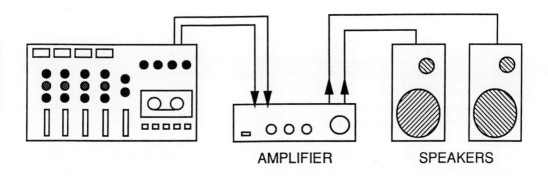

AMPLIFIER   SPEAKERS

This is how to do it: on the portastudio find the LINE OUT, or STEREO OUT sockets. On the hi-fi amplifier look for the TAPE IN, LINE IN, or AUX IN sockets. Use these sockets to connect the portastudio to the amp. When you try this, make sure the power is OFF, the volume controls are DOWN, and the speakers are connected to the amplifier. Keep the volume controls down until after you've switched the power on because many amps will make a loud 'bump' or 'thud' when they are switched on, and this sound may damage the speakers.

If you have no hi-fi then you could connect your portastudio to an instrument amp (for example, a guitar amp and speaker). This type of amp will not be stereo but mono, so you may need to use a special lead that combines the left and right outputs from the portastudio to the one single input on the amplifier.

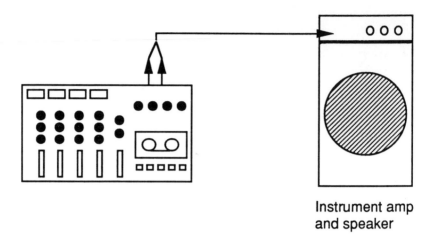

**Instrument amp
and speaker**

If the instrument amp has two inputs, check that one isn't a lot louder than the other. Some portastudios have a special output socket that sends a mono version of the sound to an instrument amp. Look for a socket marked TAPE CUE OUT.

It is possible to buy very small speakers, with amps included, that are specially designed to work with portastudios. These are called Powered Monitor Speakers. Manufacturers include Fostex, Yamaha, and Boss.

2 Using headphones to hear the portastudio

Even if you decide to use the portastudio through your hi-fi, headphones are essential in a lot of multitrack recording. Suppose you have recorded a rhythm track and now you want to record the saxophone part over it. The saxophone player obviously needs to hear the rhythm track but, if you replay it over loudspeakers, the microphone will re-record it with the saxophone. If you decide later that you need to turn up the saxophone track, the rhythm track will increase in loudness too.

Headphones allow the musician to hear the tape without its going over the loudspeakers.

Headphones are also very useful if you need to practise without disturbing other people, or if you don't want anyone else to hear what you are recording!

Headphones for portastudios should be stereo (you can tell by looking at the jack plug on them – stereo jack plugs have two plastic rings at the tip instead of the single ring found on mono plugs).

Although it is sometimes useful to have a volume control on the headphones, in general the fewer moving parts headphones have, the longer they tend to last.

A headphone splitter box (sometimes called a Headphone Distribution Box) allows more than one person to plug headphones into the same socket. The simplest type is a 2-way splitter where one headphone jack plug divides into two sockets allowing two pairs of headphones to feed from the one output. Headphone splitter boxes plug into the headphones socket of a portastudio but split the headphone signal six or more ways, enabling that number of people to plug headphones into the splitter box and listen to the same thing.

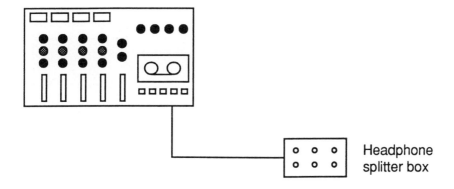

Headphone
splitter box

When using splitters it is important that all the headphones have the same Impedance otherwise some will be much louder than others. The impedance of headphones is always shown on the box, and is measured in Ohms. The higher the impedance the quieter the headphones will be and the less chance there is of plugging them in to a loud signal and damaging the ears.

Equipment Management and Storage

The philosophy behind the portastudio is that the studio can be taken to the musicians instead of the musicians going to the studio. Ideally the portastudio should be seen as a resource available to groups of pupils at all times. In reality few schools will have the resources to provide a portastudio for every group of six to eight pupils, and the teacher will need to organise work to enable recording facilities to rotate around groups.

Unfortunately, the more electronic equipment is carried around the more likely it is to be damaged, especially within a busy secondary school.

Perhaps the most flexible solution is to keep the portastudio connected together with a headphone splitter box and headphones on a portable two-tiered trolley. The trolley should have an integral 4-way mains block into which the portastudio should be plugged, and other instruments such as a drum machine and synthesiser could be housed on the lower tier, permanently connected to the inputs of the portastudio. The trolley might also house effects units, and even a small low-powered amplifier with loudspeakers.

This arrangement has worked well in schools where the accommodation is on one floor and enables the equipment to be safely and speedily brought to pupils with almost no setting up.

For extra security it is possible to fix to all items of equipment self-adhesive 'loop plates' through which a security chain may be passed. This will not only deter daytime theft, but has the added advantage of keeping the equipment on the trolley if someone trips over a microphone cable connected to the portastudio!

Provided a secure store room is on the same floor, the trolley can easily be kept there when not in use.

An alternative, if less flexible approach, would be to house the portastudio in a secure cupboard in one of the rooms available to the music department. Ideally the machine should be plugged in and connected to headphones or amplifier and speakers. Pupils wishing to use the machine would need to move themselves and their instruments to this particular room.

Pupils should not be expected to plug the machine into the mains themselves, and should need to make the minimum connections between the portastudio and instruments, microphones, or headphones.

If the machine does have to be carried around the building, or between different floors, then a strong carrying case (called a flightcase) ought to be considered as this will help prolong the working life of the machine.

CHAPTER 16

LOOKING AFTER YOUR PORTASTUDIO

As you use your portastudio two things start to happen to the tape heads that record and replay your tapes. They start to get dirty because, as the tape moves over the heads, it leaves behind a small deposit of the magnetic coating used to record the sound. Also they begin to pick up 'electronic dirt' in the form of magnetism, which will ruin any recording if it builds up. This will happen on normal stereo cassette recorders too, but because the size of the heads on a portastudio is so small this dirt will cause trouble very quickly. In fact the recording may start to be impaired after only a few days' heavy use, so weekly cleaning of the tape heads would be a good investment of someone's time!

Keeping the tape heads clean and demagnetised is very important if the machine is to give years of useful life and about half the 'faulty' machines sent back to suppliers turn out to have problems related to cleaning!

There are other parts that would benefit from a clean, too. These are any metal tape guides, and the rubber pinch roller. Here's where you will find them in relation to the cassette tape:

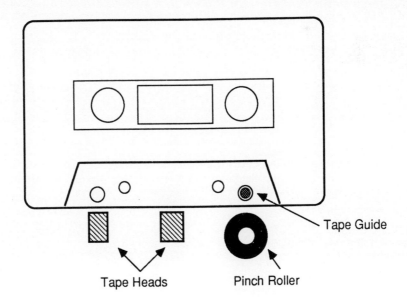

Tape Guide

Tape Heads   Pinch Roller

These are the things which need to be done if the portastudio is to stay in good working order:

Weekly cleaning of the heads and tape guides.
Occasional cleaning of the rubber pinch roller (the little black wheel on the right).
Half-termly demagnetising of the heads to get rid of any build-up of magnetism.

And here's how to do them:

Cleaning
To clean heads and tape guides, either buy a Tape Head Cleaning Kit consisting of cleaning fluid and cotton buds from a hi-fi shop (but *not* a cleaning cassette, which works like sandpaper on the heads!) or buy a bottle of Isopropyl Alcohol and a packet of cotton buds from the chemist. You should keep this locked away for obvious reasons, and you may need to sign the poisons book when you buy it.

To clean the pinch roller you will need rubber cleaner fluid from the hi-fi shop, or, if finance is tight, try spit!

How to clean the Heads and Tape Guides
Switch the power off.
Open up the cassette cover – if it will come off, remove it.
If there's a cassette inside, take it out.
Dip the cotton bud into the cleaning fluid and gently rub it over the two heads.
If lots of dirt comes off, repeat with another bud.
Repeat this process for the metal tape guides.

How to clean the rubber Pinch Roller
Switch the power on.
Open the cassette cover and remove any cassette.
Don't use Isopropyl Alcohol: it eats rubber for breakfast!
Dip the cotton bud into the rubber-cleaning fluid.
Press PLAY and hold the bud lightly against the right-hand side of the rubber roller which should now be turning round.
Dry the roller by holding a dry bud against the right-hand side of it.

Demagnetising
Buy a Demagnetising Cassette such as the TDK HD-01 from a hi-fi shop.
Note   There are strange objects called 'Demagnetisers' on the market, which until recently provided the only means of removing the build-up of magnetism on the tape heads. Unfortunately these can actually make matters worse if they're not used properly. If you touch the heads with one, or the power switches off half-way through the operation, the heads may be totally ruined.

How to Demagnetise
Play the demagnetising cassette as instructed.

What do you do when something doesn't work? Resist the urge to push every button in sight! What you need to do is locate exactly where the problem lies and this is best achieved by checking through the set-up from start to finish.

For example, suppose you are trying to record using a microphone and listening with headphones but nothing is working. The problem may be the microphone, the mic cable, the portastudio, or the headphones.

Try to check them all independently. Maybe the headphones are broken: try plugging them into a keyboard. Check the mic and lead by plugging them into an amp that you know is working. Here is a list of common problems, each with a problem-solving checklist.

Always check the meters. These will often give you a clue, but check what they are actually showing. Many portastudios allow you to decide what the meters respond to, for example a live input, or a previously recorded track.

1 We're trying to record with a mic but there is no sound

Look at the meters. If they seem to be responding to sound from the microphone, then skip the first checks and go straight to the second set.

If the meters show nothing check the following:

Is the mic switched on?
Is the lead working?
Have you plugged it into the correct input socket?
Is the input switched to the MIC setting?
Do you need to turn up the GAIN or TRIM control? (Chapter 2.)
Is the correct fader up?
Is the master fader up?

If the meters are responding, check the following:

Have you sent the channel to the correct track? (Chapter 2.)
Is the track Record Select switch on?
Are the headphones plugged into the correct socket?
Is the headphone level on the portastudio loud enough?
Are the headphones monitoring the CUE/MONMIX? If so, check the CUE/MONMIX volume controls.
Are there volume controls on the headphones themselves?

2 We're trying to record an electronic keyboard but there is no sound

Look at the meters. If they seem to be responding to sound from the keyboard then go straight to the second set of checks.

If the meters show nothing check these first:

Is the keyboard switched on with its volume control up?
Have you used the correct output socket on the keyboard?
Have you plugged it into the correct input socket?
Is the jack lead working?
Is the input switched to the LINE setting?
Is the correct fader up?
Is the master fader up?

If the meters are responding:

Have you sent the channel to the correct track? (Chapter 2.)
Is the track Record Select switch on?
Are the headphones plugged into the correct socket?
Is the headphone level on the portastudio loud enough?
Are the headphones monitoring the CUE/MONMIX? If so, check the CUE/MONMIX volume controls.
Are there volume controls on the headphones?

3 There's no sound when we play the tape back

Immediately check that you have switched the track Record Select switch off. You may actually be erasing your recording!

Turn up all the CUE/MONMIX controls and set the headphones to monitor the CUE or MONITOR MIXER.
Check the CUE/MONMIX volume controls.
Turn up any volume controls on the headphones.

Try checking the meters. Set them to show the individual tracks. You may need to find the TAPE REPLAY switches too.
If you still hear nothing it's possible you never recorded at all. Perhaps:

You kept the PAUSE button on.
You didn't press RECORD.
You didn't set the track Record Select switch.
Using the Buss method, you sent the input to the wrong track.

4 The recording is very faint

If you are listening back on headphones using the MONITOR MIX, check the volume controls and any volume controls on the headphones. If the recording is still very quiet then perhaps:

The mic was too far away.
The MIC GAIN (TRIM) control was not high enough. (Chapter 2.)
You are using the wrong sort of microphone. (Chapter 13.)
The channel fader wasn't high enough.
You are using a cheap old tape. Check the tape is a good-quality chrome (Type II).

5 The recording contains tracks we don't want

First find out which track(s) the unwanted sound is on. If you find it on its own separate track, simply turn that track off, or erase it.

If the unwanted sounds are mixed up with your recording (on the same track), then either:

You used the Buss method to record but panned the unwanted material to the recording track by mistake. (Chapter 2.)
The heads haven't been cleaned and the erase head is not totally erasing previous material. (Chapter 16.)

6 The recording has a distorted sound

The input level was too high: check the GAIN (TRIM) controls are not turned up too much. (Chapter 2.)
The headphones are turned up too high: turn down the headphone monitor control.
The playback is too high: turn down the master fader.

7 The recording includes too much outside noise

Close all doors and windows; if possible, ask the outside noise to shut up. Now try again!

Place the microphones nearer to the sound source and re-record.

The problem will be worse if you are using an omni-directional microphone instead of a directional one. (Chapter 13.)

Here are some possible ways of reducing outside noise:

Try using a noise gate if you have one. It will get rid of outside noise when the instrument or vocalist is silent. (Chapter 14.)
Try some acoustic screens. Perhaps these could be built within the school as part of a design project. Cardboard around the mic may help.

8 The recording includes too much tape hiss

Check the NOISE REDUCTION is on and you are using a chrome tape.

Tape hiss is a problem when the input signal is too low. If recording an electronic instrument try turning its volume control to full. (To be on the safe side turn the input fader or trim control on the multitrack down first.) If recording with a microphone either place the mic nearer the sound source or check that you are using the right type of mic (low impedance not high).

9 Not all the tracks are playing back

Using the MONITOR MIXER, check that all four volume controls are turned up.

Using the MAIN MIXER, check that all the channels are set to TAPE REPLAY.

Alternatively, you may be listening on mono headphones or stereo headphones with one side not working.

CHAPTER 18

BUYING A PORTASTUDIO

Buyers of portastudios are spoilt for choice, there are at least a dozen models available at any time ranging in price from around £250 to £1,000.

Your budget may narrow the choice, but it's a good idea to clarify exactly which features are important to your pupils before looking at different models. For example, ease of use and ruggedness may be more important than sound quality and lots of features.

If possible, ask the advice of local schools already using a portastudio in the classroom.

Finally, keeping in mind the pupils who will use the portastudio and the situations in which it will be used, here are some points to consider when deciding which machine to buy.

Is it Classroom-proof?

How robust does it seem?

If you can, send the demonstrator off to make some coffee before gently pulling the knobs to see if they come off!

Do the faders feel firm and stable?

Does the case look well made?

Does it plug directly into the mains? If not:

What type of power supply unit does it use?

Does the supplier have a replacement power supply unit in stock?

Can the portastudio be run from batteries in an emergency?

How Easy is it to Use?

Does the portastudio look well laid out?

Can the demonstrator explain clearly how it records?

Does the manual look readable?

Is there a separate MONITOR MIXER? (Some machines use the auxiliary controls as monitors. This can make life more complicated.)

How Good is the Sound Quality?

If possible, ask the demonstrator to record something simple on the machine. Beware of pre-recorded demonstration tapes; often many hours of work together with a bank of additional expensive equipment is lavished on these tapes.

Indicators to good sound quality are Dolby noise reduction (as opposed to DBX), and a high speed facility (3¾ inches per second as well as the standard 1⅞ ips.)

WHAT FACILITIES DOES IT HAVE?

How many inputs are there? (How many instruments or mics can you plug in?)

Can all inputs take microphones? (Some machines only allow two input channels to be used with microphones. The rest of the channels can be used only with electronic instruments.)

How many tracks can it record simultaneously? (This will vary between two and four.)

Does it have equalisation (tone controls) on every input?

Does it have auxiliary sends? (Useful if you have any effects units such as reverberation.)

Is there a SYNC facility? (Useful if you want to link your portastudio to a music computer or sequencer.)

WILL IT WORK WITH MY EXISTING EQUIPMENT?

Will it easily connect to your hi-fi system? (Which output sockets should you use, can the supplier provide a connecting lead?)

What audio leads do you need to connect your keyboards to the portastudio?

PRICES/SERVICE

Finally, always compare the prices, delivery time and repair facilities of several dealers. Usually educational suppliers will be able to offer substantial discounts.

Some suppliers will offer a complete package including microphones, headphones, and a headphone splitter box. This can be very useful, but check on the quality of the extra items.

Reproduced and printed by
Halstan & Co. Ltd., Amersham, Bucks., England